THE POWER OF
MUSIC THINKING

THE POWER OF MUSIC THINKING
LISTEN, TUNE, PLAY, AND PERFORM

HOW MUSICAL ANALOGIES HELP US
TO CO-CREATE A SOUND BUSINESS

BIS PUBLISHERS
BORNEOSTRAAT 80-A
1094 CP AMSTERDAM
THE NETHERLANDS
T +31 (0)20 515 02 30
BIS@BISPUBLISHERS.COM

WWW.BISPUBLISHERS.COM
WWW.MUSICTHINKING.COM

ISBN 978 90 6369 630 6

WRITTEN AND DESIGNED BY CHRISTOF ZÜRN

FINAL EDITING: GILLESKE KREIJNS, BUREAUTXT.NL
PROOFREADING: JOHN LOUGHLIN
DTP SUPPORT: LUC DINNISSEN, STUDIO DS
CUE FIGURE PICTURES: EEFJE VOETS, ITS COVER

TO MY GIRL GROUP

PROLOGUE

LIVING IN A SOUND BUSINESS

I grew up in an entrepreneurial household; my parents had a joinery with more than 50 employees. The workshop was just 100 meters from our family house, which was also the drawing office and showroom. Family and business affairs were always mixed, especially at the lunch table, where three generations would discuss the daily business of school, work, and what happened in the world.

Our workshop had three entries. On the left side was the entrance to the foreman's office – this was the door my father (entrepreneur, creative, innovative) often used when he took clients for a tour of the workplace. My mother (accounting, finance and people) entered the building through the right door to chat with the employees or bring them a fresh *Brezel* when they had to work overtime. The middle door was open most of the time; through here, materials were brought into the joinery, and you could hear the sound of joinery machines coming from the workplace.

There were high-pitched, short sounds from circular saw machines, and a fascinating deep drone from a big wood planer — a machine to bring the wood to the right thickness. The sounds of the woodworking machines mixed with birdsong and other sounds of labour. This was the soundscape that impacted me when I was a kid. Years later, when I started my working life there, I got to experience the joinery business from many different perspectives, and I always used the middle door.

Later, when I played in several bands and studied musicology, I found the same patterns: listening, seeing, and sensing from different perspectives at the same time. A holistic view always incorporates many perspectives. As a creative lead, service designer, and management consultant in many companies – from start-up and governmental organisation to multinational – I am always recognising patterns and different viewpoints and relating them to the whole.

So, in retrospect the three doors, the many perspectives of an organisation, and the diverse roles, personalities, business styles, and music genres I have come to know stood at the cradle of Music Thinking: connecting different views in meaningful collaboration for a sound business.

Christof Zürn

I wrote this book for you,
the leader who knows that followers can be leaders and
leaders become **followers**.

and for:

the **entrepreneur** in need to connect and sync all the
different approaches and activities in business;

the **service designer** who is making innovative design
sprints but sees how the one benefiting the people most
does not make it to implementation;

the **expert** looking for meaningful collaboration while
working with various departments and several systems;

the **brand manager** who feels that the brand experience
should be the same as the customer experience and the
employee experience;

the **change agent** who is struggling with all the different
signals trying to get the change message across;

the **music lover** who wants to solve wicked problems.

Have a look at the Music Thinking Framework on the inside of the front cover. This is the essence of the book in one picture. You can fold it out and use it while reading.

The Music Thinking Framework is a creative invitation to think from diverse perspectives simultaneously and get inspired to work in meaningful collaborations above silos. It helps you to integrate methods and mindsets like Agile, Design Thinking and Service Design with Branding and Organisational Change. It aids in rethinking your business, product, service, or organisation with the guidance of interconnected perspectives and dynamic phases inspired by the sheer endless possibilities of music in the broadest sense.

This book is in black and white. Please colour it with your personal experiences and thoughts.

 This icon indicates an exercise

OVERTURE

FROM SQUIGGLE TO SINE

Let's rock this!

Are we in sync?

I noticed a pattern.

Let's jam about this.

Let's pull all the plugs.

What is the tone of voice?

We should orchestrate this.

Does this resonate with you?

Let's make a remix of all this.

But what is the right cadence?

We are in the Gig Economy now.

We have to improvise a solution.

Have you ever noticed that when people work together, they often use expressions like 'Let's rock this!' 'Are we in sync?' 'I've noticed a pattern.' 'Let's jam about this.' 'We need to improvise a solution.' 'What is the tone of voice?' 'We should orchestrate this.' 'We have to find the right rhythm.' 'Let's pull all the plugs.' 'Let's make a remix of all this.' 'I hope this will resonate with our customers.'

The pattern behind these expressions is that they all have a music context, whether the person using it is aware of it or not.

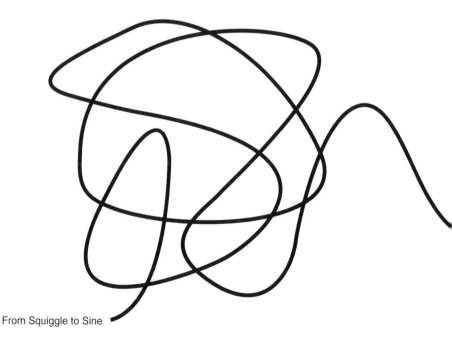

From Squiggle to Sine

What if we were to dig a little deeper into what is behind these concepts and the rich repository of meanings, ideas, and inspirations? Music – like business – can be international and local and it can affect you on an individual as well as on a group level. What possible analogies are there between what happens in music and what happens in business?

This book is about recognising a pattern in one system and realising it in another system to create meaningful collaborations. To do this, I have developed a flexible framework that incorporates all the ingredients that come into play when connecting the analogies between music and business.

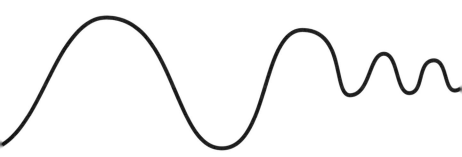

At first, this might feel chaotic, but when you just start and listen deeply you will start to recognise structures, pulse, beat, rhythm, cadence, and patterns that inspire you to new perspectives of doing.

Finding a new direction from the chaos, like a sine wave emerging from the noise, is a musical and transformative way out of the disorder.

And because simplicity and complexity are best friends, I will first show you the complexity of the model and then take you by the hand to make your own start in waltzing with complexity and starting to find the right cue, rhythm, and instrument for your endeavour. In short, this is how you get from a **squiggle to sine**.

The book consists of five acts and a backstage chapter with soundbites, playlists, and a kind of glossary.

Act I The Universal Power of Music states that music can be more than just a stimulant or the personal experience of a musical taste. We dive into the ingredients of music in the pattern repository, we look at how we listen to music and what analogies there are with business. We learn that every musician is doing four things at the same time. Listening, tuning, playing, and performing. In the Music Thinking Framework I call these the 'four phases'.

Act II A Framework Based on Musical Principles explains all elements of the Music Thinking Framework you'll find on the inside of the front flap – step by step. Then I will introduce you to the Unanswered Question template that can be downloaded from musicthinking.com. Act II concludes with the suggestion to read this book with a certain perspective, either individually or from a team or organisational perspective.

Act III Take the Cue Train introduces the six cues: JAMMIN', EMPATHY, PERSONALITY, SCORE, AGILITY, and REMIX. These are central directions or focus points. We learn about the central questions that are connected to the cues and the fact that all cues have two sides: a leading and a following side. Following this, we'll dive deeper into every cue in seven chapters.

Because everything is connected, I invite you to find your own way and flip from cue to cue in the way you find most appealing. All cues connect in a system and make sense when you understand all of them.

Act IV Let's Play Together uses the knowledge from the previous chapter. We'll see how the cues work together and how they can form triangles with names like co-creativity, strategy, research, production, and three perspectives on experience: service experience, brand experience, and organisational experience.

Because in the 21st century it is hard to differentiate between service and product, I use the word 'service' throughout the book with the idea that it is also a product.

Act V Every Business is Dynamic introduces the extra dimension of dynamics and how we experience the phases – listening, tuning, playing, and performing – differently. The way the cues and instruments work together depend on circumstances related to time and simultaneousness. This will affect the overall practical experience.

These dynamics find their analogy between a musical genre style and styles of business.

The *Backstage* chapter dives deeper into transformative techniques in using analogies and finding patterns. We also find examples of the AND-musician, people who are experts in one field and also musicians who have the power to use this duet as an analogy – deliberately or unconsciously.

You are encouraged to make your own connections, analogies, and conclusions based on who you are and how you listen – to music, to yourself, your family, the society you live in, nature, your team, and your business.

While many books present a diverse array of examples and studies that might be interesting but not applicable for your purposes, I have taken the opposite approach. I focus on the essence and the analogy of what music – and therefore Music Thinking – can offer.

On certain pages you will find links to the Music Thinking website with cases, as well as more materials to explore and download.

ACT I

THE UNIVERSAL POWER OF MUSIC

What do Lady Gaga, David Guetta, Beyoncé, Drake, Farinelli, Ed Sheeran, Peter Brötzmann, Mozart, Dolly Parton, Djalu Gurruwiwi, Patti Smith, Nusrat Fateh Ali Khan, Eminem, Ravi Shankar, Leonard Bernstein, The Beatles, Fairuz, Queen, Miles Davis, Liu Fang, Metallica, the New York Philharmonic, the Ukulele Orchestra of Great Britain, and Karlheinz Stockhausen have in common? They all move people with their music.

Although they are from different times, geographies, and musical genres and practices, all of them have their own special creativity, personality, performance, way of working, and audience. And there are many more examples – examples that might resonate with you.

The power of music lies in its ability to speak to all aspects of the human being – the animal, the emotional, the intellectual, and the spiritual. Music teaches us, in short, that everything is connected.
Daniel Barenboim

Music can change your mood, give you personal relief, intellectual pleasure, give you a sensation of joy, a feeling of empowerment, a feeling of being safe, a sense of belonging, and much more.

But music can be more than just the experience of a personal musical taste. There are many books that relate music to life. In his novel 'The Glass Bead Game', Hermann Hesse combines music with the ancient I Ching, meditation techniques, and western mathematics – all in a utopian 25th-century setting. At the start of the novel, Hesse describes an ancient Chinese story that draws the relation between music and the state of a country.

Therefore, the music of a well-ordered age is calm and cheerful, and so is its government. The music of a restive age is excited and fierce, and its government is perverted. The music of a decaying state is sentimental and sad, and its government is imperilled.
Hermann Hesse

There are many research papers that have found interesting facts about how music affects us. For example, what listening to and playing music does in our brain, what our musical taste says about our personality, and how musicians work together in a follower-leader constellation.

To move people is the essence of organisations. Music in the broadest sense moves people. So, how might we learn from this big field of possibilities to make our business better?

If you see a pattern in one system, it is easy to see it in another system. Music Thinking principle

What do we hear and how do we listen?

When hearing a song, some people get up and start dancing. Others are attracted to the melody and sing along. And some people lean back, put on their headphones, and enjoy the quality of the sound or try to understand the structure of the composition. So how we listen and what we take from the music depends on a variety of dimensions.

In its essence, music consists of sound characteristics. Think about motives and parameters like rhythm, tempo, melody, harmony, volume, texture, dynamics, form, sound, timbre, or spatial experiences.

When these characteristics are combined and repeated, we can recognise patterns. We hear them in songs with particular arrangements, orchestrations, and different styles.

But how we listen to music is also essential. There is a big difference between listening to a song on the car radio with your friends on a holiday trip or listening alone with headphones to a vinyl record. We experience the songs and styles in services like records, radio, playlists, smartphones, and concerts at festivals or clubs.

PATTERN REPOSITORY

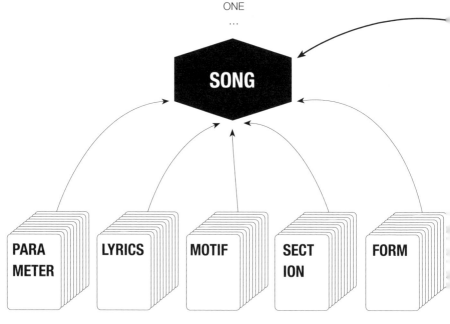

ACE OF SPADES
KYOREI
TAKE FIVE
LA DONNA È MOBILE
DER HÖLLE RACHE
WALKÜRENRITT
BOHEMIAN RHAPSODY
ONE
...

SONG

PARA METER	LYRICS	MOTIF	SECT ION	FORM

STRUCTURE	LANGUAGE	PATTERN	INTRO	AABA
SPACE	LITERATURE	LEITMOTIEF	VERSE	FUGUE
TIMBRE	POEMS	GROOVE	CHORUS	SONATA
VOLUME	ONOMATOPOEIA	HOOK	BRIDGE	AD LIBITUM
HARMONY	...	DRONE	SOLO	12 BAR BLUES
MELODY		GUITAR RIFF	MOVEMENT	JAZZ STANDARD
TEMPO		BEETHOVEN'S 5TH	OUTRO	REQUIEM
RHYTHM		WE WILL ROCK YOU	FADE OUT	SYMPHONY
		...	...	OPERA
				SOUNDSCAPE
				...

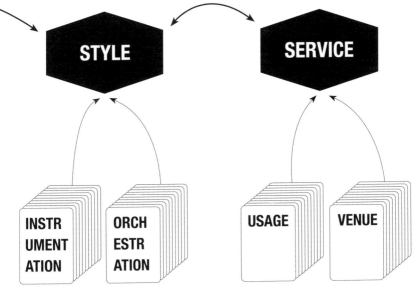

HIP HOP
METAL
POP
JAZZ
ELECTRONIC
EXPERIMENTAL
TRADITIONAL
FOLK
CLASSICAL
...

PLAYLIST
STREAMING
MIXTAPE
BROADCASTING
TV
RADIO
DEVICE
CONCERT
...

STYLE

SERVICE

INSTRUMENTATION

ORCHESTRATION

USAGE

VENUE

VOICE
GUITAR
BASS
CELLO
VIOLIN
SYNTHESIZER
PERCUSSION
WOODWINDS
BRASS
STRINGS
...

SOLO
DUO
TRIO
QUARTET
QUINTET
SEXTET
SEPTET
OCTET
NONET
TENTET
BIG BAND
SYMPHONY ORCHESTRA
GAMELAN ORCHESTRA
WAGNER ORCHESTRA

CD
VINYL
ALBUM
45 rpm SINGLE
RADIO FORMAT
JINGLE
TV SHOW
PODCAST
SONIC LOGO
PRODUCT SOUND
...

HOME
STAGE
JAZZ CLUB
AMPHITHEATRE
OUTDOORS
OPEN AIR STAGE
CONCERT HALL
OPERA HOUSE
FESTIVAL
...

Although these elements define the music, we don't hear them one by one; we listen to the whole mix of ingredients and connect them to our personal story and context – like the first time we heard a song, the identification with the lyrics, a sentiment, celebration, state of mind, or a memorable moment.

Those who wish to sing, always find a song.
Swedish proverb

 ## PATTERN REPOSITORY EXERCISE

Let's try to find analogies between music and your business. Have a look at the Pattern Repository graphic and think about the following questions:

What are the parameters of your endeavour?
What are the instruments you use?
How can we hear them in your final product?
What is your song, your style, your service?
What is your story?
What connects your business to your audience?
What are your patterns of success?

Listen & tune & play & perform

As a musician, you listen, tune, play, and perform every day.

First, to get input you sense and listen deeply; then you tune in and make meaning out of the inputs you have gathered. You play while exploring possibilities to perform on stage. While you are on stage, you listen to your fellow musicians, and you tune in to what they play. You explore, learn, and sync instantly. You are not just playing; you are performing in front of an audience that is listening to you. And here we come full circle: you are listening and tuning, and the audience is doing the same.

These four phases overlap differently depending on the genre – be it hip hop, classical music, opera, jazz, rock, pop, or dance. Classical music seems more like a step-by-step process; it starts with writing the composition, then we have the rehearsal, and eventually the performance. In jazz, everything is happening simultaneously: listening, instant composing, tuning in to the new material and playing with it while performing live on stage.

During these phases, musicians give each other signs to co-create inside the given timeframe. These small cues are interconnected to an array of different instruments and together they build a living system.

But this living system does not only exist on stage during a concert. There are so many more people involved in a music experience; think about what happens before the performance and after, what has to be done to let everyone perform in time and how to keep the audience happy and safe?

Because music – like business – is highly involved with people, technology, and overlapping systems, there are many analogies we can draw inspiration from and apply to our daily life. The flexible and dynamic phases, the ongoing iterations with recurring moments of high performance have their parallel in the business world. It is worth looking at the universal patterns, principles, and relations in music and to see how we can recognise them in a business context.

For example, listening can consist of all data you collect as a company, like information about your stakeholders, their (latent) needs, context, and behaviour. Tuning makes sense of the data relating to the company's purpose and then decides what to do. Playing is exploring, learning, and creating new possibilities, and performing is getting it to the point in the given time at the right moment.

ACT II

A FRAMEWORK BASED ON MUSIC PRINCIPLES

Organisations need to create, deliver, and live in a meaningful collaborative work sphere to provide services that people really need, want, buy, and use. But many organisations struggle with bridging silos, management layers, and having people work together effectively. That's why changing the business is a constant challenge for any endeavour.

The Music Thinking Framework is designed to tackle these challenges. Let me explain the different layers of the Music Thinking Framework: six cues, suggestions for instruments, four phases, and diverse dynamics.

Cues to start, focus and connect
JAMMIN', EMPATHY, PERSONALITY, SCORE, AGILITY, and REMIX are the essential focal points of meaningful collaboration and creation – I call them cues.
These cues relate to each other, give each other input and output, and work in an everlasting loop or iteration from JAMMIN' to REMIX. That's why there are repeat signs on the left and right side of the framework with the cues in the centre.

Instruments for intervention
Every cue can use different tools and methods; in Music Thinking, we call them instruments. The instruments come

from diverse areas that, at first sight, might have little in common, like Agile, Branding, Service Design, or Systemic Thinking. For example: systemic mapping, stakeholder mapping, persona, customer journey mapping, brand values, guiding principles, the Golden Circle by Simon Sinek, the business model canvas, kanban boards, rapid prototyping, and serious play methods.

All the instruments are associated with one or more cues. So, the context, the relation, and the fact that the instruments correlate and that people relate with the same instruments above silos make them meaningful.

Overarching phases and dynamics

Four overarching phases enclose the cues with their instruments: Listen, Tune, Play, and Perform.

Listen stands for getting new information in the broadest sense. Tune stands for making decisions based on insights from all kinds of information. Play stands for challenging insights and creating solutions. Perform stands for putting it all together to get the best possible outcome based on all the wisdom and feasibility you obtained during the other phases.

Listen and Tune are the phases that make up the

challenge space. In the challenge space, we are not looking for solutions; we focus on the challenge that we need to understand before coming up with ideas and solutions.

Play and Perform are the phases that build the solution space; here we work on ideas that might be a possible solution and produce an outcome that can be shipped in the given time.

Please note that the Listen phase is active in all other phases. That is because our ears are 'always on'; they continuously receive information – like a business is getting quantitative and qualitative data all the time. This means at any given time we get new information, and we can act upon it.

The dynamics will be affected by the amount of listening in the other phases and how the business acts upon this with the cues and instruments. You'll learn more about that in *Act 5 Every business is dynamic*.

For every project, team, and organisation, there is one big question: **How can we continually keep listening to the relevant information and act upon it?**

Iterations for change on three levels

You can use Music Thinking on three levels: individual, team, and organisation.

At the first level, you think and act as a leader and follower. You connect your perspective with the different views of your environment. You are creating and making choices for yourself and others. Sometimes you lead by following, and sometimes you follow by leading.
At the second level, you operate from a team or group perspective. All members co-create with dynamic leadership and followership to work on the common goal.
The third level is the perspective of an organisation.
You operate from a multi-stakeholder perspective, their environment, and the society we all live in.

Taking it back to the musician's experience: you can experience the three levels, for example, as a bass player in a band playing at a prominent international festival during a tour. It's the interrelation between the person, the instrument, the team, and the higher purpose. Many levels come together with all their complexity. So best is to choose one level at a time and combine the others later.

It is best to start and iterate step by step. For example, you can start with a sketch for one instrument – in

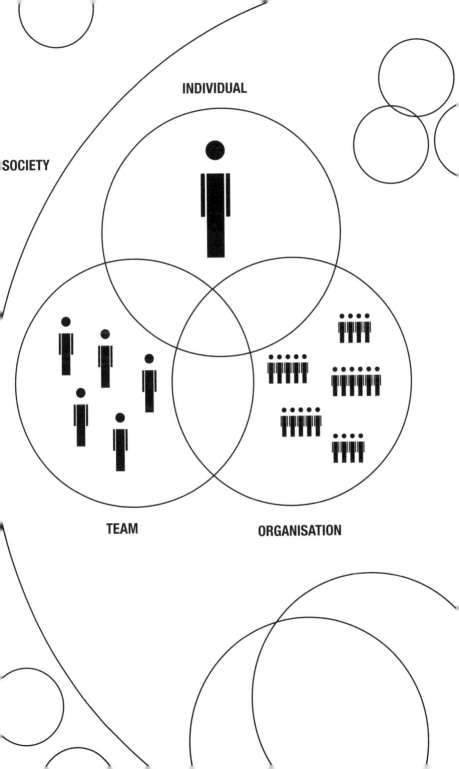

INDIVIDUAL

SOCIETY

TEAM

ORGANISATION

business, this could be a customer profile or persona – and refine it later in one of the iterations. If you give the sketch a name like 0.1, everybody understands that this is good enough to work with now and will be improved later. It's like learning to play an instrument and mastering it over time.

In this way, repetition and iteration are fundamental ways of working inside the framework. That's also why there are repeat signs on both sides of the Music Thinking Framework.

How this all plays together will be described in the following chapters.

 But before we dive deeper into the cues, we need a starting point for our iterations. We need a (wicked) problem, a challenge, or a nagging unsolved puzzle that needs change to be solved.

It helps if you read this book with an Unanswered Question in mind, whether it be from an individual, team, or organisational point of view.

Start with the Unanswered Question

We all know that most client assignments start with
a problem or a solution in mind. The main focus is to
tackle the problem or to just fix the solution. The biggest
challenge for meaningful collaborations is to check if
the assumption on the situation or solution is right. It is
also important to see if the research and the insights
of the research are evenly distributed throughout the
organisation or just the 'crazy idea of the most extravert'.
That's why it is essential to mutually agree on what is what
I like to call the Unanswered Question.

To my ears, a 'problem statement' or 'design challenge'
sound too solution- or product-oriented. This often
stimulates short-term quick fix sprint thinking.

That's why I prefer to call it the Unanswered Question; it
gives the company more space to explore what exactly
is going on. It also helps to connect short-term and long-
term thinking about whether an iteration, innovation, or
transformation is needed.

There is a three-part structure that is connected to the six
cues.

The 'Unanswered Question' is a short orchestral piece
composed by Charles E. Ives. I invite you to listen to it and
try to think about an Unanswered Question of your own.
Firstly, we need to face the facts and describe input from

our stakeholders and combine it with our company values. It starts with Given the fact ...

The second part starts with How might we: 'How' stands for 'we don't know the answer yet', 'might' for 'we even don't know if it is possible', and 'we' stands for 'this is a group effort and needs meaningful collaboration'. It is very important that we don't frame this 'how can we', because this would mean we already know that it is possible, and we just need to brainstorm a solution. The 'How might we' keeps us in the challenge space.

The third part describes a possible outcome, the goal we want to achieve. The reason why we are exploring and creating this makes it meaningful.

UNANSWERED QUESTION STORMING

Do an 'Unanswered Question storming' of about 50 variations together with your team. First start in silence and then share your unanswered questions. Get a feel of what the words mean and how they send us in certain directions.

Tip: For every variation use a new template; this will help you to see the impact of the differences. I am sure there will be one that is worth exploring to get all participants on the same page.

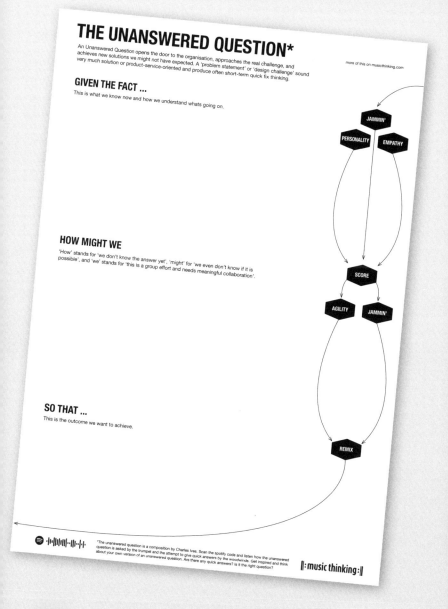

THE UNANSWERED QUESTION*

An Unanswered Question opens the door to the organisation, approaches the real challenge, and achieves new solutions we might not have expected. A 'problem statement' or 'design challenge' sound very much solution or product-service-oriented and produce often short-term quick fix thinking.

more of this on musicthinking.com

GIVEN THE FACT ...
This is what we know now and how we understand whats going on.

HOW MIGHT WE
'How' stands for 'we don't know the answer yet', 'might' for 'we even don't know if it is possible', and 'we' stands for 'this is a group effort and needs meaningful collaboration'.

SO THAT ...
This is the outcome we want to achieve.

*The unanswered question is a composition by Charles Ives. Scan the spotify code and listen how the unanswered question is asked by the trumpet and the attempt to give quick answers by the woodwinds. Get inspired and think about your own version of an unanswered question. Are there any quick answers? Is it the right question?

‖: music thinking :‖

Download this template from musicthinking.com

HOW DO YOU LISTEN?

TO YOURSELF?
TO YOUR TEAM?
TO YOUR BUSINESS?
TO SOCIETY?

ACT III

TAKE THE CUE-TRAIN

JASPER and the six cues

Let me introduce JASPER, an acronym for JAMMIN', AGILITY, SCORE, PERSONALITY, EMPATHY, and REMIX.

These are the essential focal points of meaningful collaboration and creation – I call them cues.

We will learn that JASPER can also permutate to JEPSAR, EPSJAR, RAJEPS, etc. But JASPER is easier to remember. So, in short, here is the basic formula for Music Thinking:

$$MT = \|: JASPER :\|$$

The word 'cue' has multiple meanings. It is an action or gesture, used to prompt another event in a performance. It can be a reminder, a hint or suggestion, but also a direct call to action.

In classical music, for example, we have the cue by the conductor to signal the exact point of coordination based on a precisely notated and rehearsed music score.

For an opera singer, a cue can be two different things. Firstly, from the conductor to sync with the music – out of the orchestra pit below. Secondly, from the prompter – out a stuffy wooden box at the edge of the stage – giving the singer the opening words of each phrase a few seconds early. The opera singer needs to make sense of these two different types of cues, based on the score and the rehearsals with the people giving the cues.

In standard jazz, the chord changes guide the music. All the players know the lead sheet with the melody and harmonic signs. So, if the soloist plays a particular motif, like the melody of the song, he cues that he wants to go back to the start. The other players understand this and move with him.

In rock music, a cue can also be found at the end of a song when the tension is high and everybody is raising his instrument to signal the very ending. One player gives the final cue to the end.

A more complex way of cueing comes from Ornette Coleman in what he calls Harmolodics. In Harmolodics, melody, harmony, and sound play an equal role in improvisation. For example, when Ornette gives a specific cue, the bands' reaction would generate new structures in sound while keeping the melody and harmony alike. If you are not used to listening to changes in sound quality or timbre, the part sounds boring because the melody and harmony do not change.

How does this translate to a business context?

In a business context, we also need a signal or impulse to call for attention in different moments. A moment to begin something new, a moment to keep on doing what we do, maybe with a different pace, quality, or direction, and moments when we have to hold our business to speed up later.

The six cues in the Music Thinking Framework fall into these very moments and they are the starting points for answering questions like,

JAMMIN'	How can we be more creative?
EMPATHY	How can we genuinely be more people-centric?
PERSONALITY	Who are we as an organisation?
SCORE	What is the best way to communicate so we all know who and why we are, how we work, and what we shall do?
AGILITY	How can we operate a more flexible and transformative business?
REMIX	How can we consistently deliver to, and continuously surprise, all our stakeholders?

Depending on the context and situation, we can select a specific cue as a pivotal change hub in a connected system. Because the cues are interconnected, they will not stand alone. They act as connectors for meaningful collaboration with the other cues.

Each of the six cues has two interwoven elements. A leading and a following side. One incorporates the other.

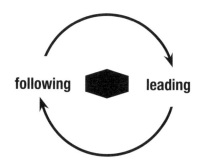

following   **leading**

You might have noticed that one cue appears in two places in the framework: JAMMIN'. That's because different kinds of creativity are needed depending on the situation. Do you require free creativity or creativity based on a given input? The former compares to a conversation with someone you speak to for the first time: you need to start the conversation and sense where it might go.
The latter compares to a conversation with someone you know well, and there is a clear expectation of where it should go. Or, in musical terms, it is like free improvisation or free jazz versus material-based improvisation like in traditional jazz. So, there is JAMMIN' before SCORE and JAMMIN' after SCORE.

We will dive into the cues one by one in the following chapters.

following		leading
to open	**JAMMIN'**	to sense
to listen	**EMPATHY**	to understand
to be	**PERSONALITY**	to become
to show	**SCORE**	to do
to explore	**JAMMIN'**	to create
to learn	**AGILITY**	to change
to deliver	**REMIX**	to live

JAMMIN' before SCORE

Use this cue to start a new endeavour, when you are in doubt, or in case of a crisis where you need to look broader than your experience.

The mind is like a parachute, it only works when it is open.
Frank Zappa

You can't rehearse what you ain't have invented yet.
Wayne Shorter

The JAMMIN' cue is very special because you can use it in both spaces in the Music Thinking Framework, from *opening up* and *sensing* in the challenge space to *exploring* and *creating* in the solution space. The connection between the two is creativity at its core.

If you use JAMMIN' at the beginning of a project, it is all about sensing information, observing, listening to emerging ideas, and collecting data from all kinds of sources. Let things unfold that are not yet there, share with others and see how they resonate.

All products and services that we see, feel, hear, smell, taste, and use are created by someone at a specific time under certain circumstances, with various intentions in mind. Most innovations came to life because someone dared to be open and move into unfamiliar territory. While in unfamiliar territory, you are most alive and alert because you are unsure of what is going on.

That's what musicians do when they start to improvise and put themselves at risk deliberately and deal with everything they sense and what emerges.

All over the world, musicians use improvisation, from Indian classical music and baroque music to jazz and contemporary music. In music, there are many examples of how improvisation was the start of exceptional work.

For example, the most significant composer of all times, Johann Sebastian Bach, was a formidable improviser on the organ. He used improvisation to shape his agility and often put his experience and the results in a composition. It was part of his creative process. Ludwig van Beethoven's 3rd Symphony, the 'Eroica' – a contest between reason and emotion – finds its start in an improvisation battle. Another example is the self-taught Italian composer Giacinto Scelsi. He improvised on the piano and gave the recordings to a transcriber who notated what he heard and set it into musical score. Later he would change the transcriptions to the final score. Improvisation and instant composing bend for the intended result.

The role of JAMMIN' before SCORE in the framework

In the challenge space, JAMMIN' operates before SCORE and has the function to open up and sense. This means looking without bias for signs of the time and open qualitative and quantitative sources. The more open you are, the more likely you are to have more ideas when you hear an idea. So, openness is a prerequisite for creativity and intelligence – connecting new things with other new things and known things.

It is about creating from a place we do not know yet – something unheard, unseen, unthought. The ability to open up to uncertainty is essential for letting serendipity happen and sensing things to come. It is also about unlearning and seeing what we (in principle) already know but have not seen yet.

JAMMIN' is the realisation of creation and it helps the other cues to diverge first, to see what is possible, and then converge to focus.
In this respect, JAMMIN' is also the most intuitive cue. It is connected to the ability to improvise.

Instruction for JAMMIN' without knowing
Open up to the new and sense what appears, share it with others, and see how it resonates. What do you hear? What does the co-creation involve? No judgment! Just play and listen without an intended result.

How to improvise
Improvisation together with others is a capability that can be learned. There are some guiding principles to keep in mind when improvising and co-creating together. These musical principles can easily be used in many business situations like conversations, meetings, and ideation sessions.

GUIDING PRINCIPLES FOR (BUSINESS) IMPROVISATION

Be open.

Co-create.

Make others shine.

Be there, be mindful, listen for intent.

Use possibilities and momentum.

Listen to the environment, to others, to you.

Recognise patterns, generate patterns,

break patterns.

Don't just react: initiate, support, respond.

Don't plan: experiment, change roles, try.

Stay in shape.

Actually, every meeting should be a jam session based on co-creative principles.

From my practice as an improviser, I know that there are moments in free improvisation where you would like to change the collective music that is going on. Because it makes sense from your position and perspective. So, you try to offer new material with the intent that the other players might pick it up. But sometimes, for whatever reason, they don't synchronise with you. And instead of insisting that the others should adopt your brilliant idea, the only chance to have a meaningful collaboration is to stop playing and listen more deeply to what is already going on. Listen to the whole and how your ideas might support the whole.
Consider this a bit of good advice for any business meeting.

What is music, and what is right or wrong?
To illustrate how music that you have never heard before can trigger a conversation here is a short story from my own experience. In the early 90s, directly after the fall of the Berlin Wall, the highest-ranking judges from the former soviet countries came for a visit to Karlsruhe, Germany. They were meeting the highest judges of Germany and the Minister of Justice to discuss how to establish a fair

way of lawmaking. For an extensive lunch buffet with approximately eighty people and their many bodyguards, our saxophone trio was hired for entertainment and discussion. The assignment was to play between the courses to entertain, create a pleasant atmosphere, and trigger their conversation. And hell, we did!

We played three free improvised pieces using all possible sounds that you can evoke from a saxophone. We mixed it with dynamic rhythms, reminiscent of jazz standards, and some experimental squeaking solos.

The reactions spanned from spontaneous applause to looks that could kill. After each set, there was a lively discussion about what music is, and what is right or wrong.

The organisers were pleased that the music had such an effect and after the set, we got a handshake from the minister who was happily amused and told us, 'Wow, guys, you really mixed them up!'

More info on the Jam Cards via musicthinking.com

WHY Give participants time to sense and ground themselves in the unknown.

MATERIAL Music Thinking Jam Cards or any other cards with visual, sonic, or other triggers.

DESCRIPTION Participants work solo and silent with headphones or earbuds. They scan and listen to musical examples, flip through trigger questions and inspirational quotes. They make notes about anything that comes to their minds.

HOW DOES IT WORK

1. Spread the cards on a surface, alternate between backside and frontside.
2. Let all participants wear headphones and give them the instruction to browse through the cards and note anything that comes to their minds.
3. Take one hour and let the participants work
   20 minutes solo and silent to pick two cards,
   20 minutes in duos to share and
   20 minutes to discuss in a quartet.
4. Present to the other groups and discuss.

You can use Serendipity Lab in an ideation phase as extra trigger.

Download the templates from musicthinking.com or take a piece of paper, fold it down the middle, and write JAMMIN' on top of the fold. Write 'to open' on the left and 'to sense' on the right.

Use this cue to start a new endeavour, when you are in doubt, or in case of a crisis where you need to look broader than your own experience. Collect and generate questions. Select possible instruments and activities that might help you to move forward.

Here is a suggestion of instruments that work well with this cue.

Unlearning
Deep Listening
Pattern Writing
Jam Cards
Free Improvisation
Unstructured Play
Unanswered Question Storming
Question Storming
Lego Serious Play

TO OPEN

JAMMIN'

TO SENSE

Questions to ask yourself:

What is our bias or blind spot?

Is our product or service used in an unintended way by some consumers?

How can we sense needs before they become obvious?

What is going on? What have we not seen, heard, felt, smelled, or tasted yet?

What is emerging?

Three steps in 60'   **1.** Start solo and silent with your own template. 10'
2. Discuss in duos and share your thoughts, connect and collect. 20'   **3.** Share insights in full ensemble and make connections with the other cues. 30'

This is about ideas, information, opening up, sensing and collecting data from many sources.

to open to sense

to explore to create

And the driving force of creativity, exploration, and creation based on the input from other cues.

to listen to understand

Empathy is the people-centred cue to see with the eyes of your stakeholders in their context and environment. Empathise and search for insights that matter. The two sides are listening and understanding.

to be to become

The cue to work from the heart of your organisation. Work from your why and brand values to the holding space you provide for your stakeholders. That's why this cue has two sides: to be and to become.

to show to do

The cue to visualise your decisions in the way that everyone has a 'lead sheet' of how to operate. The two sides of this cue are to show and to do. This means you need to have a vision and clear instructions on how to reach this.

to learn to change

The cue to decide how to work together in which constellations and when to do what. The two sides of this cue are to learn and to change. Together with Jammin', this is the realisation duo.

to deliver to live

The cue to getting it all together under the given circumstances based on the other cues. The two sides of this cue are to deliver and to live. There is a time when you have to deliver and to make iterations based on all the other cues.

musicthinking.com

 Download this template from musicthinking.com

EMPATHY

Use this cue for any human-centered activity and service design project. Make this the cue to start and to end with.

Knowledge speaks, wisdom listens.

Jimi Hendrix

The eye should learn to listen before it looks.

Robert Frank

EMPATHY

to understand

to listen

Now it's time to leave your current position and look at things from a different angle and distance. What does the world look like from the perspective of one of your audience members? What kind of people impact your endeavour?

What do they hear, feel, think, say, and how are they connected to society, nature, and you? How do your actions impact them? How might they impact your efforts? First listen, and then try to understand their context to empathise from this point of view and search for insights that matter to them. Understand the field of different stakeholders and contexts and look for as many perspectives as possible.

Every musician knows they are not alone on stage. Musicians listen to the co-creators they perform with and to the audience that is listening to them. For musicians, everything starts with listening, listening to music they cherish and find interesting, listening to friends and family, co-workers, people on the streets, in clubs, on the internet and the news to integrate what they hear into their music. Players do not just play music; they sense and recognise other people and their perspectives. They then invent systems of ideas, songs, products, and experiences that have an impact on others. You could say that making music and attending musical experiences allow a person to connect with others, to understand different contexts and feel more human.

Maybe that's why musicians start initiatives like 'The virtual concert' a fundraiser featuring performances by Lady Gaga, The Rolling Stones, Taylor Swift, and more. And in former times, the events 'Do they know it's Christmas', 'We are the World', and 'Live Aid' brought together musicians and audiences from all over the world to join a live event and raise funds for the force of good.

The role of EMPATHY in the framework

The function of the EMPATHY cue in the Music Thinking Framework is to listen and understand the whole context of a challenge without any bias. There is a need to zoom in and listen closely, focus on what is really being said, and sense the meaning behind the words.

Sustainable change needs empathy. The EMPATHY cue begins with listening. If we are empathetic, we are listening not only with our ears, but with our entire bodies and awareness.

We also take in all information visible, non-visible, audible, non-audible, physical, digital – we are listening with our total capacity of being. We listen to what people say and what it might mean to them. We get to their (latent) needs, which they may not even be aware of yet.

If we don't listen deeply, we might not understand the essence and make decisions based on assumptions just because they make sense to us at that moment. Here, listening is also a de-risking factor, because it can help us to avoid wrong decisions.

How can we listen more deeply and act profoundly?

Listening and understanding mean collecting information and data from everything audible, plus changing the perception and seeing the whole from many different perspectives. In this sense, EMPATHY is much more than just people-centred because, in the context of people, there is also their environment that influences people's (latent) needs and behaviours. We see the person not just as a single entity, but we understand the person's role in the systems that she is operating in.

For example, you can't just hear a sound and say, 'oh, yeah, it's a bird'. We listen to what the bird call might mean and how this connects with his surroundings, with human beings, and with the environment. If you listen deeply, you move yourself to the other side and listen from that perspective, in this case, the bird's view. You see and hear the field he and you are in. It is not just compassion for the other, it is opening up to the connected field and beginning to understand it from different perspectives simultaneously. New patterns appear and reveal the different roles, relations, and systems that impact the individual and the associated context.

To learn deep listening, find your inspiration in nature and everything that surrounds you. Listen to sounds that appear with your full attention and focus. You might also like to listen to music you have never heard before, preferably with headphones or during a concert.

For example, a contemporary composition that uses space as one of the dominant parameters, Like 'Gruppen für Orchester' (Karlheinz Stockhausen), 'Terretektorh' (Iannis Xenakis), or 'Sonic Genome' (Anthony Braxton). You will be encouraged to walk around during the show to experience different qualities of sounds in different positions. Focus on what appears and don't listen for recognition, listen for the unheard, listen for serendipity – the unexpected fortunate discovery.

Although it looks like a lot of empathy would add extra complexity, as a matter of fact, it is the opposite: EMPATHY helps us to understand complexity as long as we are open to detect and recognise unseen patterns and systems and compare them with our known patterns and systems. That will show us the way to a possible solution.

We need to empathise with every stakeholder so that we can see the whole from their perspective. We listen with our whole mind and body while walking in their shoes, looking with their eyes, or hearing with their ears. But we don't stop there; we zoom out again, visualise the patterns, collect the different multifaceted views to shape a systemic picture of our shared field and challenge. How do we do this? We map the found patterns and experiences to discuss and show them. We make sure that everyone in our business can understand them and connect them with their own experiences. The culture of empathic documentation should include all levels and all possibilities in your endeavours to create a picture of understanding and to show where you are in the moment.

We use this multi-stakeholder picture as input, and we show it in the SCORE together with the input from the next cue: PERSONALITY.

Download the templates from musicthinking.com or take a piece of paper, fold it down the middle, and write EMPATHY on top of the fold. Write 'to listen' on the left and 'to understand' on the right.

Use this cue for any service design project. Make this the cue to start and to end with.
Collect and generate questions. Select possible instruments and activities that might help you to move forward.

Here is a suggestion of instruments that work well with this cue.

Four levels of listening in Theory U
Quantitative Data Collection
Qualitative Data Gathering
Context Mapping
Stakeholder Mapping
Value Network Mapping
Reality Persona
Journey Mapping
Systemic Mapping
Doughnut Economics

TO LISTEN

EMPATHY

TO UNDERSTAND

Questions to ask yourself:

How do we listen to our business?

With whom are we listening together?

Who are we excluding from our listening?

How can we genuinely be more people-centric?

What does it take to listen properly and to understand?

Three steps in 60'   **1.** Start solo and silent with your own template. 10'
2. Discuss in duos and share your thoughts, connect and collect. 20'
3. Share insights in full ensemble and make connections with the other cues. 30'

This is about ideas, information, opening up, sensing and collecting data from many sources.

to open **JAMMIN** to sense
to explore   to create

And the driving force of creativity, exploration and creation based on the input from other cues.

to listen **EMPATHY** to understand

Empathy is the people-centred cue to see with the eyes of your stakeholders in their context and environment. Empathise and search for insights that matter. The two sides are listening and understanding.

to be **PERSONALITY** to become

The cue to work from the heart of your organisation. Work from your why and brand values to the holding space you provide for your stakeholders. That's why this cue has two sides: to be and to become.

to show **SCORE** to do

The cue to visualise your decisions in the way that everyone has a 'lead sheet' of how to operate. The two sides of this cue are to show and to do. This means you need to have a vision and clear instructions on how to reach this.

to learn **AGILITY** to change

The cue to decide how to work together in which constellations and when to do what. The two sides of this cue are to learn and to change. Together with Jammin', this is the realisation duo.

to deliver **REMIX** to live

The cue to getting it all together under the given circumstances based on the other cues. The two sides of this cue are to deliver and to live. There is a time when you have to deliver and to make iterations based on all the other cues.

musicthinking.com

PERSONALITY

If your challenge, project, or programme has to do with organisational change and (internal) branding, make this cue your starting point.

Find out who you are and do it on purpose.
Dolly Parton

We identify with each other, I see myself in my fans and my fans see themselves in me. I call them little monsters because they are my inspiration.

Lady Gaga

to be

to become

When you feel and recognise the flow and tension between who you are and who you want to become, you might experience high-energy moments. Every action you take is related to what people have experienced with you. It makes the difference if people trust you as a person, your brand, or your organisation in any further step.

The why question, why do we live, why are we here, seems complicated in life and in business. Many companies struggle with a clear definition or even a strong feeling about why they are operating, their more profound meaning of life, and what they bring to the society they live in. If it is only making money and providing people with a (temporary) job, this might not be enough to differentiate from the competition or to save the planet.

So, the question of who you are and how people can recognise you in our ever-changing world is critical before making decisions.

Followership and Leadership
If you listen to Miles Davis albums like 'Birth of the Cool', 'Kind of Blue', 'Miles Smiles', 'Bitches Brew', 'Tutu', or 'Doo-Bop', you encounter many different sounds, styles, genres, and musicians. Although the songs are very different, you can hear and feel Miles' charismatic

personality in all of them. How is it possible to develop, change, innovate, and co-create new musical styles for over more than five decades? Miles did 405 recording sessions in his lifetime and played with 577 musicians – aside from rehearsals, try-outs, jams, and concerts.

An essential factor in his approach to musical innovation was the recruitment of young musicians.
Miles was looking for musicians with a fresh attitude, a connection with the younger generation and the will to try out something new. Either Miles or one of the band members came up with an idea or a rough sketch that would form the base for further development. Most of the musicians talked about Miles as the 'best listener who ever led a band'; he heard what everybody else was playing, and with his voice and the ability to show new possibilities, he was the glue that made it sound like a whole band. It was Miles' personality that that connected and inspired all the personalities to create something new. 'Everyone who played with Miles feels a bond with each other,' says Herbie Hancock. Playing with Miles was extraordinary and inspiring. It had a permanent influence on the people he worked with. That's why nearly all musicians that played with Miles later became famous musicians and bandleaders themselves.

But Miles' personality did not only inspire musicians. There is an interesting story about one of the most famous restaurants in New York: Eleven Madison Park. In 2011 the restaurant started to use a younger and slightly less reverend tone to reinvent itself; it earned the restaurant a rating of three and a half stars out of four from the *New York Observer*. The famous critic Moira Hodgson called the elegant but sober restaurant 'not dull anymore'. The critic's only note was that the restaurant could use 'a bit of Miles Davis'. This resonated deeply with young chef Daniel Humm, and together with his team he researched 'the eleven words that were most often used to describe Miles Davis'. Because they already knew Miles Davis' music and personality, they could easily link it to their culture. In the kitchen, they hung giant posters of Miles Davis and the eleven words that characterise him to inspire everyone to work in this spirit and create an atmosphere that reflects their values and culture.

The role of PERSONALITY in the framework

The PERSONALITY cue works from the heart of your organisation, from your why and values to the holding space you provide for all your stakeholders – internal and external.

The PERSONALITY cue influences and incorporates everything a business is: the purpose, the strategy,

INTRO Tell the story of Eleven Madison Park.

PARTICIPANTS You can do this alone, or even better, with your team.

DESCRIPTION Begin silent and solo. Everybody has a piece of paper. Take some time for yourself and think about music. Think about what kind of music gives you wings and makes you fly. Write down your thoughts. If you have one musician in mind, research what attributes define this musician – write down how other describe the music, the personality.

Take a big poster and write the musician's name at the top, then the attributes that describe the music or musician, and five songs that incorporate the characteristics.

Walk around the exhibit of posters together and answer the question: **What words define us, our personality, our business, our service? What musician is missing in our business?**

OUTRO After that, share the eleven attributes from Eleven Madison Park: cool, endless reinvention, inspired, forward-moving, fresh, collaborative, spontaneous, vibrant, adventurous, light, innovative.

the products and services, and the gut feeling of what people think about you as an organisation or brand. So, where a brand strategy is in balance with its culture, the brand experience equals the consumer experience and the employee experience. For example, brands like the outdoor brand Patagonia are in sync with their stakeholders on nearly all cues. The company pledged to donate one percent of its sales (or 10 percent of its profits, whatever is higher) to grassroots environmental organizations, a practice that continues today.

The PERSONALITY cue in the framework is vital to remind us about why we are doing things. If the PERSONALITY cue is not connected, we might design, develop, and deliver a product or service to clients that does not fit the organisation, or the other way round. People who know the brand might not buy it because it does not resonate with the brand experience.
For example, if a budget airline in the pandemic decides to offer train rides, people might like and use the train offers. Still, they would not buy it because they couldn't believe that the airline also purchased trains and offered the same budget service.
It is hard to change when your purpose is single-minded and focussed only on money. So, for change you need to know who you are and who you want to be.

The PERSONALITY cue has two sides: to be and to become.

On the one hand, to be, what the organisation is and whatnot. But also, on the other hand, what should be changed to stay relevant for clients, employees, consumers, and other stakeholders.

PERSONALITY and the other cues

In *Act IV Let's play together,* I will explain how the cues relate to each other. But I will give you a sneak preview of a connected description. It helps if you have a look at the framework on the inside of the front flap PERSONALITY needs input from EMPATHY to understand people, their environment, and how the organisation fits with their needs and personality. The job of PERSONALITY is to give the right input to SCORE and the mix of what the organisation stands for and what should be changed in the future. Because AGILITY gets input from SCORE, it creates a feedback loop for learning and real change in comparing this input with the possibilities of realisation. Meaning, everything you learn and change affects your personality, not what you just say.

It is not fake it till you make it, but make it till you be it.

Download the templates from musicthinking.com or take a piece of paper, fold it in the middle, and write PERSONALITY on top of the fold.
Write 'to be' on the left and 'to become' on the right.

If your challenge, project, or programme has to do with organisational change and (internal) branding, make this cue your starting point. Collect and generate questions. Select possible instruments and activities that might help you to move forward.

Here is a suggestion of instruments that work well with this cue.

Why (of the Golden Circle)
Purpose
Brand Values
Vision, Mission
Guiding Principles
Leadership & Followership
Aspirational Persona
Holding Spaces
Storytelling

TO BE **PERSONALITY** TO BECOME

Questions to ask yourself:

Who are we as an organisation?

Why might people follow me, or us?

Why do we exist?

How do our customers, employees, the society, and the planet connect with our purpose?

Where do we come from and where do we want to go?

Three steps in 60' **1.** Start solo and silent with your own template. 10'
2. Discuss in duos and share your thoughts, connect and collect. 20'
3. Share insights in full ensemble and make connections with the other cues. 30'

This is about ideas, information, opening up, sensing and collecting data from many sources.

to open to sense
to explore JAMMIN to create

And the driving force of creativity, exploration and creation based on the input from other cues.

to listen to understand

Empathy is the people-centred cue to see with the eyes of your stakeholders in their context and environment. Empathise and search for insights that matter. The two sides are listening and understanding.

to be to become

The cue to work from the heart of your organisation. Work from your why and brand values to the holding space you provide for your stakeholders. That's why this cue has two sides: to be and to become.

to show to do

The cue to visualise your decisions in the way that everyone has a 'lead sheet' of how to operate. The two sides of this cue are to show and to do. This means you need to have a vision and clear instructions on how to reach this.

to learn to change

The cue to decide how to work together in which constellations and when to do what. The two sides of this cue are to learn and to change. Together with Jammin', this is the realisation duo.

to deliver to live

The cue to getting it all together under the given circumstances based on the other cues. The two sides of this cue are to deliver and to live. There is a time when you have to deliver and to make iterations based on all the other cues.

musicthinking.com

 Download this template from musicthinking.com

SCORE

Use this cue in combination with all the other cues.
All cues relate to SCORE.

The score is not the music and the strategy is not the service.
Music Thinking principle

SCORE can be two things: a pilot's dashboard and a musical score with enough detail to give direction and to synchronise all the different perspectives.
Music Thinking principle

The two components, *to show* and *to do*, are the essence of SCORE. The score cue is in the middle of the Music Thinking Framework and serves as a pivot between challenge and solution space.

If you look into the meaning of the word score, there are many fields where it is used: in sports, business, school, gaming, film, and music.

On the one hand there are graphics, dashboards, and high scores, while on the other hand there are musical scores. The difference is that the first one is about showing what the score is – this could be an actual score or a score that one might reach in the future. In the second one, we see a detailed instruction readable by trained musicians on exactly what to do to evoke a certain sound. In short, the first is 'to show' and the second 'to do'.

The role of SCORE in the framework
SCORE in the Music Thinking Framework has a very broad meaning, it is not only the visual score but also everything that is in some way defined as the way of working and performing for the best result.
SCORE unites the knowledge of the past with instructions to design the future. So, the function of SCORE is to make clear who we are, who we might want to become, what we

want to achieve, and what everyone involved should do to reach the collective goal.

The score is a zero point in the framework and is the endpoint of *to show*. It gets input from EMPATHY, PERSONALITY, and JAMMIN'. It is the result and synthesis of all that we have started, sensed, listened to, understood, who we are and what we want to become. But just to show this synthesis – or a future ambition you would like to reach – is not enough to move forward. To explore, create, learn, change, deliver, and live in a meaningful collaboration space, we need understandable directions of what and how everybody involved should do to guide us through the solution space.

So, all the choices that we make in scoring our business will have a direct influence on the dynamic of interactions and flow.

Because musicians have been in the scoring business for ages, it is interesting to look at different practices of how they designed these directions and how much instruction is needed by the ones who realise the score and transform it into an experience.

What can we learn from the way musicians use a score?

There are predictions that Spotify will have more than 100 million tracks of music in 2022. According to the Every Noise at Once website, there are 5701 genre styles of music as of December 2021 and still counting. And then there is music that is in some way genre-fluid, using different kinds of styles. Every song, every musical experience might have another way to organise the way they play together. This means there are endless ways to create a musical score.

In the Pattern Repository graphic in Act I, we see different characteristics that make a song, a service, or style. So, if we look closer into the broader genre styles, some recurring and combined characteristics form new patterns that could inspire our thinking about working together. I will oversimplify some of them on the following pages to accentuate what they have in common, revealing new patterns, and invite you to think this further in a personal, society, or business context.

Essential patterns in genre styles

Here, I give you an oversimplified description of basic patterns in a selection of music styles to inspire and to compare with your own patterns – as a leader, as a team or organisation.

Classical music

In classical music, an individual – the composer – is writing down his ideas based on inspirations in an explicit, detailed instruction called the musical score for others – the orchestra musicians. They have to execute what is written in the score to create the intended sound the composer had in mind. The quality of the music depends on two significant factors. Firstly, the training of specialists and the capability to play what the composer has determined. Secondly, the will to synchronise with a conductor who is also the visionary, trainer, coach, judge, and 'chief listener' to bring this instructed idea of the music performance to life. The organisation of a concert or recording of a classical piece is to do everything needed to create this unique sensory experience.

'There are two qualities that are missing in classical music. The first is the ability to improvise. In classic music we have become slaves of the written notes, we are so preoccupied with being "historically correct". ... The second is the energy that is expressed in for example rock music, which is sometimes missing in classical. The negative side of that kind of music is that it is unnecessarily primitive in harmony and rhythm.' Daniel Barenboim

GENRE STYLES

canadian singer-songwriter
post-screamo
background piano
rap conciencia
cool jazz
tra
canadian trap
swedish hip hop
pop reggaeton
chillwave
cana
indonesian indie
dreamo
chillwave
pi
traprun
polish pop
baton rouge rap
bubblegum dance
compositional ambient
cancion melodica
drift phonk
desi hip hop
country dawn
dream
cumbia 420
korean r&b
lo-fi jazzhop
scorecore
rockabilly
meme rap
beatlesqu
german drill
rap espanol
latin worship
turkish hip hop
grupera
new rave
austral
r&b en espanol
modern indie pop
progressive rock
funk metal
pop nacional
vocal house
rock nacional
dream smp
dutch pop
worship
puer
jam band
ska argentino
vapor twitch
electronic trap
anime
sad lo-fi
toro
uk contemporary r&b
dancehall
viral rap
neo mellow
regional mexican
amber pop
gen z singer-songwriter
yacht rock
modern alternative rock
trap soul
jazz pop
taiwan pop
nz pop
trap
emo
ca
cumbia pop
g funk
sufi
lgbtq+ hip hop
jazz
spanish p
spanish pop rock
big room
indie pop
spanish po
post-disco
dutch rap pop
norteno
canadian pop
cali rap
ccm
rap francais
new wave pop
bass trap
detroit hip hop
folk
christian music
motown
nu jazz
children's music
cantautor
alternative hip hop
pop punk
pop rock
c
dmv rap
freak folk
progressive electro house
nyc rap
banda
pop
ove metal
bossa nova
nova mpb
country rock
german pop
gaming edm
chanson
rain
atl hip hop
c-pop
punk
trap latine
candipop
brazilian edm
new jack swing
uk dance
k-pop girl group
sertanejo
funk
sertanejo pop
classic italian pop
trap triste
turkish trap pop
conscious hip hop
sert
gruperas inmortales
show tunes
trap argentino
post-teen pop
francoton
rap r
aby
glitchcore
dutch edm
glam metal
indonesian pop
house
new romantic
uk drill
funk paulista
polish trap
world worship
boy band
east coast hip hop
dance rock
ir
afro r&b
kleine hoerspiel
modern bollywood
j-rock
la indie
plugg
turkish rock
r&b
bolero
indietronica
rofuturism
jazz funk
christian alternative rock
argentine rock
rap metal
neo so
russian alt pop
brostep
new americana
j-pop
electro
stralian indie
chillhop
aesthetic rap
reggaeton flow
contemporary countr
swedish trap pop
acoustic pop
nu metal
synthpop
pop edm
heffield indie
neo-psychedelic
florida rap
social media pop
swedish pop
opm
tropical
cumbia sonidera
barbadian pop
west coast rap
art pop
rumba
thrash metal
baroque pop
lo-fi beats
mexican pop
sad rap
anthem worship
indiecoustica
escape room
gla
instrumental lullaby
video game music
german trap
canadian
alter
indie anthem-folk
deep groove house
funk rock
classic
indie rock italiano
power metal
turkish 1
turkish folk
rap calme
industrial metal
regg
musica popular colombiana
partyschlager
latin viral pop
deep german h
tennessee hip hop
kore
deep tropical house
industrial rock
mexicar
uk alternative pop
rock nacional bras
complextro
etherpop

pagode novo

classic bollywood

blues   pop argentino   french rock

lo-fi product   shimmer pop   bubblegrunge

deep regional mexican   rap marseille   shiver pop   neon pop punk

p hop   norwegian pop   skate punk   filter house   double drumming

russian trap

north carolina hip hop   anime rock   nigerian pop   southern soul

o trap queen   eurodance   russian pop   old school thrash   panamanian pop

op   polish hip hop   garage rock   symphonic rock   sophisti-pop   german metal

hardcore hip hop   otacore   vapor soul   dfw rap   philly rap   madchester

urbano espanol   modern country rock   italian adult pop   indie garage rock   hype

bedroom pop   pixie   indie rock   comic   hollywood   brazilian hip hop   bow pop

latin arena pop   stomp and holler   pop flamenco

riter   forro   funk carioca   chicago rap   brill building pop   new orleans rap

country road   german hip hop   punjabi pop   southern

uk hip hop   country   filmi   psychedelic rock   downtempo

hop   pop r&b   classical music   uk pop   mexican hip hop   background m

reggaeton   vapor trap   queens hip hop   irish rock

mphonic music   roots rock   viral pop   deep house   german dance

o   hip hop   adult standards   permanent wave   pop soul   roots re

ap pop dance   underground hip hop   chill r&b   brazilian rock   afropop   medi

rock   mellow gold   nuevo regional mexicano   talent show   gauze pop   houston rap

hern hip hop   alternative rock   metropopolis   argentine hip hop   pop venezola

indie folk   corridos tumbados   pittsburgh rap

ock   urban contemporary   rock en espanol   vocal jazz   australian rock   la pop

tario   corrido   slap house   tropical house   mariachi   classic uk pop   cumbia v

runge   electro house   pagode   alternative metal   melodic metalcore   nueva cancio

miami hip hop   dark trap   latin rock   neo-classical   redne

trance   latin pop   rock-and-roll

ock   album rock   alt z   alternative r&b   j-poprock   spanish hip h

quiet storm   electropop   reggaeton colombiano

hop   lounge   gangster rap   hip pop   electronica   mexican rock   ohio hip hop

melodic rap   hoerspiel   french hip hop   k-pop   french pop   bachata   japanese teen p

sierreno   blues rock   new wave   british invasion   candy pop   indie pop

ne

sa   italian pop   metalcore   russian hip hop   funk ostentacao

atin alternative   britpop   ranchera   dirty south rap   german rock   italian indie pop

disco   classical   indie poptimism   mandopop   hip house   samba

op   indie r&b   desi pop   europop   australian pop   modern blues rock   post-punk

ae   progressive house   k-pop boy group   dutch hip hop   trap italiana   tamil pop   punk blu

y r&b   soundtrack   piano rock   folk-pop   texas country   nouvelle chanson francaise

new french touch

brooklyn drill   melancholia   australian dance   danish pop   german underground rap

egum pop   outlaw country   atl trap   french indie pop   latin christian   bachata dominica

asy listening   merseybeat   wrestling   socal pop punk

perreo   dominican pop   german techno   k-rap   spanish rock   trap boricua

acao

o rap latina   future bass   dutch rock   anime score

an gospel   christian rock   norwegian indie   classic canadian rock

e   trip hop   swedish electropop   white noise

focus beats   brooklyn indie

n   movie tunes   deep new americana

Rock

Rock music has no written score besides possibly some chord symbols and lyrics that indicate the basic sound and structure. All the members of the band will rehearse the structures. Every member will add his personal sound, and there will be experimentation and changes until there is a version that all of the players are content to play. This version of a song will then be played without significant changes over many years. In live performances, the audience expects the pieces to be played exactly as they are on the album.

Bruce Springsteen is a great example. The YouTube video 'Through the years pro shot' shows excerpts from several decades of Born to Run, with the underlying music unchanged. You see 40 years, different fashions, different players, different venues, the band getting older – but still the song stays the same.

Pop

Technically this might be the biggest genre where many different styles are subsumed. I will focus on one leading pattern. Pop music as we know it from the charts is highly technological and often individual. An artist, producer or DJ collects material records and mixes new material directly into a digital audio workstation. It is a process of recording, creating, changing, mixing, and doing this all over again. There is no actual score. However, the studio technique with a mixing panel and a massive variety of effects and manipulatory instruments functions as a score that can be manipulated very quickly. Changes are often made on a micro level with the focus on sound, including various remixes to work perfectly in different media like radio, streaming, CD, or vinyl.

Jazz

In traditional jazz, there is the basic idea of distinctive elements – a *lead sheet* with a melody line and harmonic symbols. It is the starting point of personal, individualistic interpretation and improvisation based on this material. There is a lot of freedom in co-creation depending on the size of the ensemble.

In smaller ensembles, like a duo, trio, or quartet there is more freedom to alter the material than in larger groups, such as a Big Band. The freedom of the improviser is mainly limited by the timeframes of a solo over a given chorus and harmony.

Free improvised music or free jazz

There is no written, visual score in free improvised music. However, the will to collectively depend on the moment and the action-interaction between the players is an unwritten principle.

Melody, harmony, and sound play equal roles in the improvisation. Sound is a very individual personal parameter with tonal quality, sonority, how notes are phrased and articulated rhythmically. The musicians need to listen to understand the changes made in different areas. New ideas develop instantly and in co-creation. The freedom of the improviser depends on the consent about the music while it is played.

Folk, world, indigenous
In much folk music, and especially in non-western music, the score is not visual but oral. For example, Indian classical music is traditionally transferred from master to student. It takes a long time of close learning and rehearsing until the student is ready (or allowed) to perform. There is no written score. The score is the master-student relationship and the tradition they play in. So, learning the score is purely listening to and playing with the master. This may also go for folk music in a broader sense, like Americana or indigenous music of a specific culture.

Interestingly, musicians often make their own instruments, like the didgeridoo in Australia, seashells in Asia, and skiffle instruments like washtub bass, cigar-box fiddle, musical saw, and comb-and-paper kazoos in America.

Generative music

You can also create your own instrument in electronic, digital music and in all aspects of computer-generated music with software instruments based on algorithms and manipulations of sound.

In ambient, computer-generated music, tiny programmes (algorithms) live in a system of rules and calculations. The algorithm itself has the function of a fluent and flowing score, based on principles where the actual outcome is open, but the sounds and the quality of interactions are limited by the algorithm.

There is some analogy to artificial or probabilistic intelligence, like 'Reflection' by Brian Eno, which plays indefinitely via an app, modulating its output at different times of the day.

My job as a composer is to set in place a group of sounds and phrases, and then some rules which decide what happens to them. I then set the whole system playing and see what it does, adjusting the sounds and the phrases and the rules until I get something I'm happy with. Because those rules are probabilistic (– often taking the form 'perform operation x, y percent of the time') the piece unfolds differently every time it is activated. Brian Eno

Make scoring a habit

SCORE is connected to all other cues in the framework. Some cues give input and shape the score, and some connect to the score for the intended outcome. There is always a need to clarify what you have found. This triggers questions and understanding.

Keep in mind the distinction between 'to show', meaning the visualisation of results or current state, and 'to do' with clear direction, especially on how to do things. The best advice for any organisation is to make scoring a habit. In an organisation, everybody needs the training to be an instant composer and to quickly share the level of understanding when there is no score or when the score is less detailed. Starting scoring everything that is in the context as soon as possible is a good idea. Any quick and direct connection with SCORE is like a melody sketch, the 'shitty first draft' or a version 0.1. This is just the beginning, and many great works of art and music began with just sketching the essence of what one has perceived. An excellent way to start scoring is to map the essence; you can do this in a classical form of visualisation. But you could also use soundscapes, a blend of tastes or fragrances, a tactile experience as significant triggers. Not only achieving an (intended) result but providing the story and narrative to meet this result makes scoring valuable on all levels of the organisation. May it be the company vision, reality or aspirational personas, the actual customer journey or employee journey, the systemic field of the stakeholders, a journey blueprint – you can turn everything into an instrument to start a meaningful conversation.

Make it a habit to listen and try to understand what kind of score is needed by the people who are doing the work and execute the score. If after a while it is clear to everybody, you can change the score together.

In modern classical music it is common that a composer works with an instrumentalist on the execution of a composition, to see what are the best ways to bring the idea of the music to life. This collaboration can lead to amendments in the score.

After this, the composition is fixed, including the extra suggestions from the instrumentalist so that others can learn to play the piece. Interestingly, there is always a recording (live or studio) to help new learners to read the score and listen to an execution of the score as intended by the composer.

So, if people in your organisation don't understand the score, change the score, and involve them in scoring.

If people still can't play the score at all, you might train them. If your score still does not work, you might be playing the wrong music for the wrong audience with the wrong players, directed by an unnecessary conductor. If you don't score you might never find out where your real challenge is.

Every business needs to decide what might be their most effective and efficient way to score. It is necessary to have a clear understanding of what kind of players there are – specialists to execute, specialists to improvise, or generalists who are highly flexible but never meet the depth of a dedicated expert. The challenge is to repeatedly listen deeply and honestly to your organisation and encourage the best player-score-fit, keeping in mind that it is not easy or quick to train an expert to become an expert in a different field.

Compare these basic ideas with how you score, lead, and follow in your organisation.

🟢 ⸱⸱⸱⸱|||⸱||||||⸱⸱⸱⸱|⸱ Open Spotify on your mobile and scan the code

Have a look at the SCORE playlist with musical pieces that all have an interesting score.
I encourage you to first listen to some pieces – even if you might not like them – try to visualise what their score might look like, what kind of instructions this music needs and then search the internet for the score. Share this with your team and discuss how scoring might give directions in your business.

Download the templates from musicthinking.com or take a piece of paper, fold it in the middle, and write SCORE on top of the fold.
Write 'to show' on the left and 'to do' on the right.

Use this cue in combination with all the other cues. All cues relate to SCORE.
Collect and generate questions. Select possible instruments and activities that might help you to move forward.

Here is a suggestion of instruments that work well with this cue.

What (of the Golden Circle)
Lead Sheet
Service Blueprint
Experience Design
Business Model Generation
Journey Operations
Conceptual Models
Brand Book
OGSM

TO SHOW

SCORE

TO DO

Questions to ask yourself:

How can we create a scoring culture and speed up decision-making?

What style or genre might have an analogy with our organisation?

What is the best way to share instructions so that everybody feels who we are, how we work, and what to do?

What level of instructions is needed?

Three steps in 60'   **1.** Start solo and silent with your own template. 10'
2. Discuss in duos and share your thoughts, connect and collect. 20'   **3.** Share insights in full ensemble and make connections with the other cues. 30'

This is about ideas, information, opening up, sensing and collecting data from many sources.

to open to sense

to explore to create

And the driving force of creativity, exploration and creation based on the input from other cues.

to listen to understand

Empathy is the people-centred cue to see with the eyes of your stakeholders in their context and environment. Empathise and search for insights that matter. The two sides are listening and understanding.

to be to become

The cue to work from the heart of your organisation. Work from your why and brand values to the holding space you provide for your stakeholders. That's why this cue has two sides: to be and to become.

to show to do

The cue to visualise your decisions in the way that everyone has a 'lead sheet' of how to operate. The two sides of this cue are to show and to do. This means you need to have a vision and clear instructions on how to reach this.

to learn to change

The cue to decide how to work together in which constellations and when to do what. The two sides of this cue are to learn and to change. Together with 'Jammin', this is the realisation duo.

to deliver to live

The cue to getting it all together under the given circumstances based on the other cues. The two sides of this cue are to deliver and to live. There is a time when you have to deliver and to make iterations based on all the other cues.

musicthinking.com

 Download this template from musicthinking.com

JAMMIN' after SCORE

Use this cue when working on solutions and when you ask yourself: how can we be more creative?

Creativity is more than just being different. Anybody can play weird – that's easy. What's hard is to be as simple as Bach. Making the simple complicated is commonplace – making the complicated simple, awesomely simple – that's creativity. Charles Mingus

I feel that Jazz is not so much a style as a process of making music. It's the process of making one minute's music in one minute's time, whereas when you compose, you can make one minute's music and take a month to compose one minute's music. Bill Evans

JAMMIN'

to create

to explore

Musicians have to make decisions on the fly while performing. It doesn't matter if it is the interpretation of a given idea notated in a musical score, a variation of it, or an improvisation based on a central theme. Musicians need to be in sync with their environment, the size and quality of the venue, the fellow musicians, the audience – and they need to sense, listen, and sync during the whole performance.

Execution and interpretation

On the 6th of April 1961, the conductor of the New York Philharmonic, Leonard Bernstein, did a very unusual thing. Before playing the Brahms piano concerto (composed in 1861) with soloist Glenn Gould, he gave a short note. He informed the audience about Glenn Gould's unorthodox interpretation of the concert it was about to hear. He explained that he disagreed with this interpretation. But because he respected Gould's seriousness and conception of the performance, he wanted to bring this interpretation to life and let the audience judge for themselves. He also raised the question: who then is the boss in a concerto, the soloist, or the conductor? The answer is: both, in the way that they have to manage together – with persuasion, charm, and sometimes threat to achieve a fresh performance of a much-played work.

The role of JAMMIN' after SCORE in the framework

We learned about JAMMIN' in the beginning and the challenge space, where we open up our mind, our thinking, to everything we might sense and feel. When we use JAMMIN' after SCORE, meaning we already know what to do, we are opening up to everything that the SCORE might mean to us. This leads to exploring all possibilities of how the SCORE can be realised.

JAMMIN' after SCORE is the driving force of creativity, exploration, and creation based on the input from all the other cues manifested in the SCORE. So, it is not free improvisation where we open up and sense what is going on; the score tells us what we should do. But how we might do this and find the best way to bring the score to life needs exploration in all possible ways. The score is not supposed to be just a dead piece of paper, but the realisation and performance of the intended music.

Don't just play the SCORE: explore first how you can bring to life what is intended in the SCORE. This means we should start creating, prototyping, and jamming our way to the best possible performance. In doing so, we learn the score and how the music might sound though we might have different solutions, like Glenn Gould and Leonard Bernstein taught us.

On the other hand, there is a creation based on directions like an idea, a purpose, or a need, derived from input from the cues JAMMIN', PERSONALITY, or EMPATHY.

The art of creation after the score is to not literally execute the directions, but first explore the best ways to do this and iterate to the qualitative best result.

Business improvisation

Improvisation in business is not free. A business always has a goal, like time-based goals, outcome-oriented goals, and process-oriented goals. It describes what should be achieved often in a specific timeframe. The question is, how might we reach that goal and what exactly should everyone involved do?

Improvisation in business is as old as business itself, with the annotation that most of the time it was used as a 'repair mode' when the intended plan did not work out, and it needed creativity, speed, and effectiveness to come up with a better solution to fix the problem.

Improvisation sometimes gets a bad name in business because it is often used by people trained in execution, not improvisation. The result is that it takes an extra-long time to fix the problem.

The problem is also that people think the plan was good, but only its execution was poor. So instead of looking at the preconditions, they blame the result.

As an analogy to this, we could imagine a classical piece of orchestral music where, all of a sudden, the score has changed or is not playable on the indicated instruments. Everybody needs to come up with their own possibilities to bend for a better result. But this will frustrate the composer, the conductor, every single member of the orchestra, and the worst: the audience.

If the score is very detailed, like in classical orchestral music, it needs a coach and visionary with a set of specialists to bring this idea to life without compromises. The goal is to execute everything the composer has created and visualised in the orchestral score – from instrumentation, orchestration, speed, melodies, harmonies to spatial arrangements and dynamics.
It is a strategic choice what exactly the business (in the role of the composer) has put in the SCORE and to decide what kind of score fits the players or what new players are needed to realise the score to music.

So, the significant thing is that improvisation works when there is a non-deterministic score with a lot of space for trained improvisers.
For example, in jazz there is a 'lead sheet' with a melody line and chord symbols. Every jazz player on the planet understands this and knows how to play this together.

THE ROLES OF A CO-CREATOR

PREPARATION: Stay in shape and know your instrument.
INTERACTION: Switch between the roles.

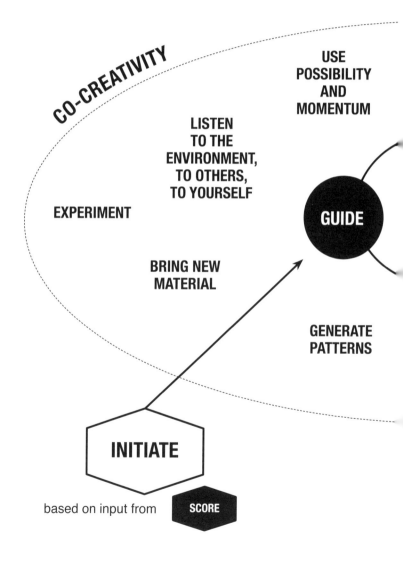

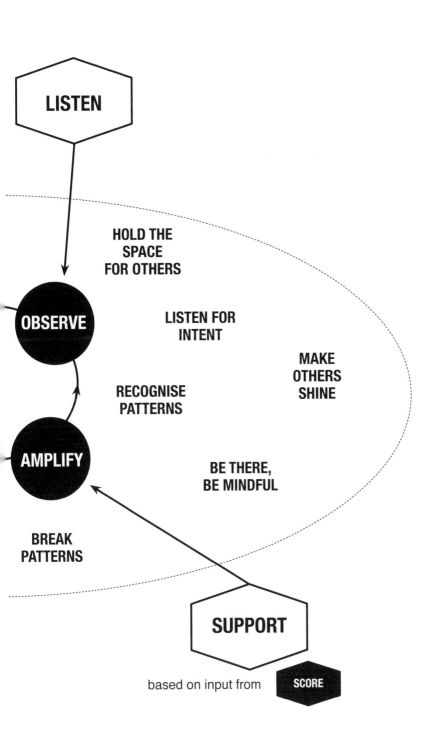

Interestingly, in baroque music, a similar approach called figured bass gave the improviser a lot of freedom to use his creativity.

Many recordings of classic jazz pieces and baroque music are extra information and inspiration for the improvisers. In this way, they learn from the written score plus the recorded performance of the score.

An interesting fact is that musicians do this a lot – also with their own recordings. In a rehearsal room or a music studio, musicians play and record and then listen to the recording to learn from themselves. They change things, play, and record again in a loop that makes the intended result and performance better. So, good music needs exploration of the possibilities, listening and reflecting in a changing iteration.

The roles of a co-creator

Improvisers – or better co-creators – don't just get up and play. To be creative in the moment, you need a lot of repetition, knowing and exploring the instrument, trying things out, and building the improvisational muscle to act on what is intended and to bend for a common result.

The setting of the co-creation is crucial. Co-creation must be inclusive. Everybody has the same influence on the outcome, whether playing actively or listening profoundly while holding the space for the others. So, everybody starts with active listening; this creates a safe space and possibilities, and signals awareness of the collective outcome.

Musicians – regardless of what kind of music they are playing – are co-creators, and they have at least three roles: listening, initiating, supporting, and listening again. Initiating brings in the material from the score, supporting is amplifying the intentions of the score, and listening is holding the space for the iteration to the intended result. That's why good co-creators switch roles between these three positions a lot.

A little business challenge
For your next team meeting, try to find answers to these questions:

Who knows the score?

Who holds the space?

Who initiates?

Who supports?

Who is switching between these roles?

Who stays in his role?

What is the iterating factor?

It will tell you a lot about your team culture.

Download the templates from musicthinking.com or take a piece of paper, fold it in the middle, and write JAMMIN' after SCORE on top of the fold.
Write 'to explore' on the left and 'to create' on the right.

Use this cue when you know your design challenge and research what your client needs, wants, would buy, and use together. Explore all (im)possibilities and different ways to solve the challenge and how this makes your brand more valuable. Collect and generate questions. Select possible instruments and activities that might help you to move forward.

Here is a suggestion of instruments that work well with this cue.

Ideation
Serious Play
Experiments Design
Experience Demonstrator
Low Fidelity Prototyping
Concept Walkthrough
Generative Design
Pattern Co-creation
Rapid Prototyping

JAMMIN' AFTER SCORE EXERCISE

TO EXPLORE   **JAMMIN'**   TO CREATE

Questions to ask yourself:

How can we explore many possibilities to get the best outcome?

How does it sound with different instruments?

How might we be more curious?

In how many ways can we interpret the score?

What clichés are limiting us?

What is determined and what is open?

Three steps in 60' **1.** Start solo and silent with your own template. 10'
2. Discuss in duos and share your thoughts, connect and collect. 20'   **3.** Share insights in full ensemble and make connections with the other cues. 30'

This is about ideas, information, opening up, sensing and collecting data from many sources.

to open   **JAMMIN'**   to sense
to explore   to create

And the driving force of creativity, exploration and creation based on the input from other cues.

to listen   **EMPATHY**   to understand

Empathy is the people-centred cue to see with the eyes of your stakeholders in their context and environment. Empathise and search for insights that matter. The two sides are listening and understanding.

to be   **POSSIBILITY**   to become

The cue to work from the heart of your organisation. Work from your why and brand values to the holding space you provide for your stakeholders. That's why this cue has two sides: to be and to become.

to show   **SCORE**   to do

The cue to visualise your decisions in the way that everyone has a 'lead sheet' of how to operate. The two sides of this cue are to show and to do. This means you need to have a vision and clear instructions on how to reach this.

to learn   **AGILITY**   to change

The cue to decide how to work together in which constellations and when to do what. The two sides of this cue are to learn and to change. Together with Jammin', this is the realisation duo.

to deliver   **REMIX**   to live

The cue to getting it all together under the given circumstances based on the other cues. The two sides of this cue are to deliver and to live. There is a time when you have to deliver and to make iterations based on all the other cues.

musicthinking.com

  Download this template from musicthinking.com

AGILITY

Use this cue to start a learning project or a cultural programme.

We train ourselves over a period of years to be able to hear rhythms and anticipate combinations of sounds before they actually happen.
Roland Hanna

Group improvisation is a further challenge. Aside from the weighty technical problem of collective coherent thinking, there is the very human, even social need for sympathy from all members to bend for the common result.
Bill Evans

The ability to act quickly and effectively based on what you desire to achieve needs two things: the capability to learn and change yourself and the things you do, and the required environment. So, it is crucial to focus on how we do things and efficiently switch between adopting new ideas and adapting a given structure.

In the last two decades, we have seen the rise of new ways to organise a business. This was triggered by rapidly changing consumer behaviour in response to new digital possibilities, new players on the market, and therefore customer expectations. The way music went from buying a CD to (illegal) download to streaming to subscription models, from owning a product to having the right to use a service.

Established businesses around the world and across a range of sectors were striving to emulate the speed, dynamism, and customer-centricity of digital players. That's why they went to Sweden to learn from a tech start-up in streaming music how they develop and iterate in the changing field of their customer needs. Then they got trained on how they could deliver in iterations of two weeks to ship their outcomes. The company was the music streaming start-up Spotify, and their way of working was called the Spotify model, where people work in squads, tribes, chapters, and guilds with a mindset derived from scrum, kanban, and other agile methodologies.

For many hierarchic companies this new way of organising work felt like the reorganisation of a Symphony Orchestra into smaller improvising jazz ensembles, asking them to perform a concert in, let's say, 'the style of Beethoven' with a changing score and no conductor. In the words of the Music Thinking Framework and what we have learned so far this means, who you are and who you are going to be are giving mixed messages to about how we should achieve the goals. Because maintaining a hierarchical organisation with all its control mechanisms, does not fit the intended self-conducting teams.

It was impossible to learn and change, because people 'learned' that the current way of working was mightier than the communication and purpose of the company's change. The leading powers were still sticking to what they always did instead of leading the change they wanted.
So, the to do of SCORE was not in sync with the behaviour of the leadership. The only thing that people learned was that the input from PERSONALITY to SCORE was not in sync with the leadership.

Stimulate to encourage change

How do you encourage the change that is needed?

An analogy. Many children in their early years get sent to music lessons to learn an instrument that often was not the instrument of their choice (a lot of wasted time to learn recorder, violin, or the piano). Parents wanted the very best for their children; they hired the best teachers and spent money on the lessons. But what they lacked was the ability to support, play together, and stimulate by leading example and experience. Although the intention was good, it did not work, and it caused more frustration than joy. Learning and adopting something new needs much more than just the instrument lesson with a great teacher. It needs a stimulating environment with engaged and active leadership as an example close by to have a collective experience and a meaningful collaboration to bring SCORE to REMIX.

So, if what is written in the score does not fit the capability of the players and the current system, then it needs a learning organisation to change it and a leadership that is helping people learn instead of trying to teach.

The role of AGILITY in the framework

The function of the AGILITY cue is to connect what the SCORE tells you to do with the delivery of REMIX. AGILITY is about learning and understanding the SCORE, organising what needs to be changed to reach the REMIX as efficiently as possible, meaning the score's realisation.

The AGILITY cue also needs to create a holding space for JAMMIN' to explore and make the best possible outcome from what the score tells you to do.
AGILITY operates in parallel with JAMMIN – active in the solution space. AGILITY and JAMMIN' together learn and explore the SCORE. This exploring and learning leads to creating and changing and finally to delivering the best transformation of the SCORE into a delivery.

AGILITY depends on the score and has the assignment to find the right constellations or ensembles to work as efficiently as possible. This facilitates the development of duos, trios, quartets into bigger ensembles.
AGILITY must help to learn the SCORE and make any changes so that the players can perform the SCORE with the best result. This means decisions of genre and constellation, like classical and orchestra, or jazz and sextet, including the consequences of orchestration and which instruments to play.

In business situations, the impact of the SCORE that got input from the PERSONALITY (why and who we are and what to become) and EMPATHY (what stakeholders need) will be felt in the AGILITY cue. That's why it is crucial to connect all the cues as early as possible, to signal the impact of the decisions made.

Scale up the playing – Ensembles in AGILITY

In classical music, depending on the programme, one musician can play in different settings like a duo or trio, or be a part of the orchestra in the same concert. They are skilled in playing their line of the composition in sync with the other players.

In smaller constellations, the players have more freedom to interpret and express the written score and to also give cues to sync with the other players. In bigger ensembles, they often double players to make the sound louder and richer. Therefore, they need to be in exact sync with each other. That's where a conductor comes into play; he is the only musician not making any sound, but he is interpreting the score, he has a clear vision what it should sound like, and he trains and coaches the musicians and helps them to sync during a performance.

Playing in different constellations also happens in jazz. Some jazz musicians also play in a big band on Monday. On Tuesday, there is a studio recording session. And on Wednesday, they teach at the music academy. On Thursday, they might rehearse with their own band.

On Friday, there is a concert. On Saturday, they might play as the sideman in a different jazz combo and on Sunday they play live on TV in the morning matinee. Various settings, different styles, different constellations, and different ways of interacting and collaborating.

Four are not four are not four

There are many ways to organise music. If there is a very detailed score, it is crucial to recruit the right people to execute it. But if you have a more open score, you might need different kinds of players. In this regard, four people are not just a quartet. Their style and way of working make a difference. It depends on the music they play and how they organise and guide their way to the best performance. So, the Fab Four – better known as The Beatles – working in the studio are completely different from the Arditti String Quartet performing the 'Helicopter String Quartet' live in a helicopter. And the John Coltrane Quartet had a way of producing the album 'A Love Supreme' that was completely different from let's say Led Zeppelin's first album.

My model for business is The Beatles. They were four guys who kept each other's negative tendencies in check. They balanced each other and the total was greater than the sum of its parts. Steve Jobs

FROM SOLOING TO ORCHESTRATION

Conductor

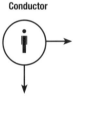

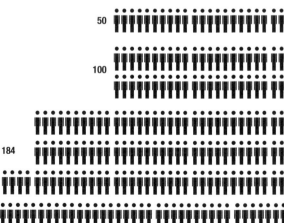

50

100

184

1000

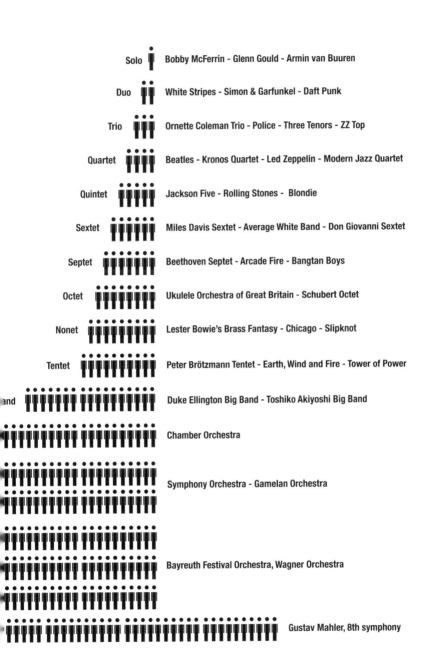

Solo — Bobby McFerrin - Glenn Gould - Armin van Buuren

Duo — White Stripes - Simon & Garfunkel - Daft Punk

Trio — Ornette Coleman Trio - Police - Three Tenors - ZZ Top

Quartet — Beatles - Kronos Quartet - Led Zeppelin - Modern Jazz Quartet

Quintet — Jackson Five - Rolling Stones - Blondie

Sextet — Miles Davis Sextet - Average White Band - Don Giovanni Sextet

Septet — Beethoven Septet - Arcade Fire - Bangtan Boys

Octet — Ukulele Orchestra of Great Britain - Schubert Octet

Nonet — Lester Bowie's Brass Fantasy - Chicago - Slipknot

Tentet — Peter Brötzmann Tentet - Earth, Wind and Fire - Tower of Power

Big Band — Duke Ellington Big Band - Toshiko Akiyoshi Big Band

Chamber Orchestra

Symphony Orchestra - Gamelan Orchestra

Bayreuth Festival Orchestra, Wagner Orchestra

Gustav Mahler, 8th symphony

Think about four people working together in your organisation. How do they work together? Are you one of them? How are they organised, like a rock band, a string quartet, a jazz band or an a cappella quartet? What makes the difference? What is their secret to success? And how do they compare to other ensembles of the same size?

The From Soloing to Orchestration graphic shows more examples of ensembles. Which ones do you know, which ones apply to the way you listen? Explore the one you don't know yet and find out more about how they sound and who they are.

Please remember that in music from approximately nine musicians, you need a conductor to synchronise and give the cues. With less than nine, one or more players will collectively sync and give cues. It makes a difference if you work with a very detailed score, a lead sheet, or just principles.

If you look at the business world and methodologies like scrum, the best size for a team is between four and seven people. For a scrum team it can be beneficial to learn from different constellations, from quartets to septets, and what it takes when there is a change in the team. Because you know the size or headcount alone doesn't make the difference.

Welcome to the festival

Scale-up does not just mean to start with a violin and then add more strings and other sections like woodwinds, brass, and percussion. Scale-up means seeing the whole field like a festival. Imagine a festival site with all its different stages and genres like jazz, hip hop, EDM, world music, classical orchestra, rock, and pop. Imagine all the other tents where people can eat, drink, come together, and sleep. And the backstage area with all the necessary means to make the festival a success.

So, scalability is more comprehensive than just the players. It is about the people who make it possible to have an outstanding performance together.

Remember the Unanswered Question at the beginning? Did you choose the individual, team, or organisational perspective?

Now map your duos, trios, and quartets that relate to it. Take a sheet of paper. Put your name in the middle. Write the names of the people you are communicating most with or have regular meetings with (how many are in the meeting?).

Start with your one-on-one relations, your duos. Connect your names to the other names with lines:

  A thick line for strong and good relations
  A thin line for weak relations
  A dotted line for distorted relations.

First map, then try to understand the perspective of your partners. How do they listen? What do they think about your listening? To whom do they listen when you are not in the ensemble?

Are there overlapping ensembles? How strong are the connections?

Are you a duo or ensemble player?

Then write down your trios, quartets, and so on. Use different colours. If it gets messy, take another sheet of paper.

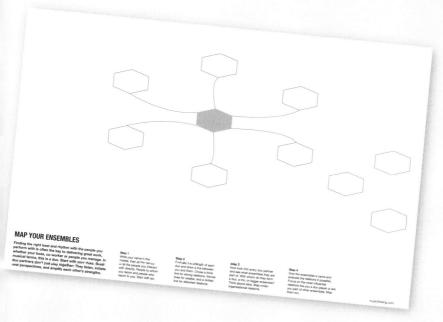

Finding the right rhythm and cadence with the people you work with is often the key to delivering great work, weather it's your boss, co-worker, or people you manage. In musical terms this is a duo. Start with mapping your duos.

Great duo partners don't just play together: They listen, tune, play and perform while initiating new perspectives and amplify each other's possibilities.

Download the templates from musicthinking.com or take a piece of paper, fold it in the middle, and write AGILITY on top of the fold.
Write 'to learn' on the left and 'to change' on the right.

Use this cue to start a learning project or a cultural programme. Collect and generate questions. Select possible instruments and activities that might help you to move forward.

Here is a suggestion of instruments that work well with this cue.

How (of the Golden Circle)
Action Learning
Team Forming
Squad Formation
Guided Improvisation
Backlog
Kanban
Service Scenario
Scrum, Agile, SAFe

TO LEARN

AGILITY

TO CHANGE

Questions to ask yourself:

What do we have to (un)learn?

What level of complexity is going on?

What is my mental model?

How can we operate a more flexible and transformative business?

Do we have the right players for the right performance?

What has to be changed?

Three steps in 60' **1.** Start solo and silent with your own template. 10'
2. Discuss in duos and share your thoughts, connect and collect. 20'
3. Share insights in full ensemble and make connections with the other cues. 30'

This is about ideas, information, opening up, sensing and collecting data from many sources.

to open **JAMMIN'** to sense
to explore to create

And the driving force of creativity, exploration and creation based on the input from other cues.

to listen: **EMPATHY** to understand

Empathy is the people-centred cue to see with the eyes of your stakeholders in their context and environment. Empathise and search for insights that matter. The two sides are listening and understanding.

to be **PERSONALITY** to become

The cue to work from the heart of your organisation. Work from your why and brand values to the holding space you provide for your stakeholders. That's why this cue has two sides: to be and to become.

to show **SCORE** to do

The cue to visualise your decisions in the way that everyone has a 'lead sheet' of how to operate. The two sides of this cue are to show and to do. This means you need to have a vision and clear instructions on how to reach this.

to learn **AGILITY** to change

The cue to decide how to work together in which constellations and when to do what. The two sides of this cue are to learn and to change. Together with Jammin', this is the realisation duo.

to deliver **REMIX** to live

The cue to getting it all together under the given circumstances based on the other cues. The two sides of this cue are to deliver and to live. There is a time when you have to deliver and to make iterations based on all the other cues.

Download this template from musicthinking.com

REMIX

Use this cue to foster an iterative culture and when your deadline is in sight.

There is joy in repetition.
Prince

I jump 'em from other writers but I arrange 'em my own way.
Blind Willie McTell

to live

to deliver

Combining and editing existing material to produce something new and offering it to an audience that needs, wants, and can afford to buy it at a particular time will always have value. This unique experience will be measured according to why, what, how, and when you deliver. To accomplish this task regularly, you need a practical mindset of iteration loops and the courage and creativity to perform at the right time with what is at hand.

The most successful musician in the first half of the 18th century was Georg Friedrich Händel. He was a serial composer, serial entrepreneur, and, today we might say, a master remixer. Händel reused material not only from his own works, but also unusually frequently from the oeuvres of other composers of his time. Maybe he did it for practical reasons like time pressure, maybe to make the borrowings more up-to-date and give them a different swing, maybe because he lacked the facility of inventing better tunes himself.

In any case, he reached the listeners of his time in full effect, from the king to the ordinary people.

Deconstructing and rebuilding tracks to suit the audience's tastes also signalled the start of the modern remixing technology in the late 1960s.

First, a few things came together: the possibilities of studio productions like Sgt. Pepper by The Beatles (who were influenced by musique concrete and electronic music from the 50s).

Secondly, the practice of local music mixers in the dance hall culture of Jamaica that stripped down instrumental mixes of reggae tunes. Like DJ Cool Herk, who mastered playing two turntables simultaneously to isolate a breakbeat from James Brown recordings like *Funky Drummer* or *Give It Up or Turn It Loose* to create a steady beat.

And thirdly, the popularisation of disco culture with the urge to keep people on the dance floor in the new clubs worldwide. There is the famous example of the Sugarhill Gang sampling Chic's *Good Times* bass riff to make *Rapper's Delight*.

Finally, there is the digitalisation and creation of new software instruments in the last 20 years. Now digital audio workstations (DAW) are available to everyone with a computer. This closes the loop that started with the studio manipulations of the early days.

To make something new, personal, and astonishing from various materials is a timeless leitmotif in musical practice. And now, with all the possibilities to remix everything, the possibilities of creation seem endless. Everything you hear is possible material at hand to move forward.

And this is not restricted to just melody. All musical entities like rhythm, timbre, and chord progressions can be mixed and remixed in new and surprising ways. See the Pattern Repository graphic at the beginning of the book; all elements and constellations are available to start making a new product or service.

A few years ago, on a Sunday morning, when I was listening to the Japanese internet station Radio Hayama – a station with only music non-stop – I heard *House of the Rising Sun* by The Animals. In the following song they played, I heard similar chords and realised that this was a reggae style cover version of the song. Surprisingly, the next song was a heavy metal song, and now, unsurprisingly, it was *House of the Rising Sun* again. In the end, the song was played ten times, but always in a different interpretation, orchestration, and style. The melody, chord changes, and lyrics were more or less the same, but the sound, speed, and the form were very different.

The so-called cover versions or interpretations of a song are fascinating. Is the song the score that, after exploring and making changes, gets a new REMIX, or is the song just a significant recurring pattern to play with? What makes the song interesting? How does the song fit the PERSONALITY? Is it just a fad, or does the

Open Spotify on your mobile and scan the code

Here is a playlist for you with more than 20 versions of House of the Rising Sun, from Bob Dylan, to Muse and Five Finger Death Punch to the London Symphony Orchestra. Listen to at least five songs in total length.

Find the differences, discuss the quality and how these versions resonate with you. What is original and what is just a blunt copy? What song of business are you covering in what style with your endeavour?

personal interpretation make the song more appealing? What is needed to hear the song from an orchestra? Is improvisation allowed?

I am not interested in collage; I am interested in revealing how, at a special moment, a human sound is that of a duck and a duck sound is the silver sound of shaking metal fragments. Karlheinz Stockhausen

Besides the obvious and easy cover versions there are other ways of remixing elements and patterns. But they are more subtle and often hidden at a micro level. They can only be revealed when analysed in detail. You can find them in contemporary music or computer music where one parameter, like the sound quality of an instrument, is changed and transformed into something new, like the rhythm of a train that changes into the rhythm of an electronic beat. For example, *Xme Symphonie remix* by Pierre Henry works with the material and patterns of Beethoven symphonies to make a composition-production of its own. Listening to this as a Beethoven fan would be a terrible experience, because it is everything but Beethoven. But if you are open to a new audible experience, it is fascinating to listen to the sounds and elements that are mixed together into something unheard, especially when you use headphones.

An extra dimension can be added if you hear this kind of electro-acoustic music via a Loudspeaker Orchestra, where the composition is live-diffused over dozens of different loudspeakers, all with their own size, volume, and characteristics. If you ever have a chance to hear Acousmonium (Paris), BEAST (Birmingham), or join a concert in the Klangdom (Karlsruhe), it is a one-of-a-kind experience.

So, the ability to invent, compose, improvise, synthesise, juxtapose, mix and remix old with new ideas, and perform this in time in front of an audience eager to listen to what you offer is the essential skill of all successful endeavours. If this matches your purpose, personality, promise, and the people's needs and expectations, you're a winner.

The role of REMIX in the framework

Every company needs to live in the present and in the future simultaneously. Every venture has to deliver what people expect from them, now. But they also have to look into the future and make the right decisions in order to stay in business and exceed people's expectations.

The function of REMIX is to foster a mindset to perform under the given circumstances that are related to all the other cues. REMIX is a point of culmination – the current iteration's temporary endpoint and the starting point for the next round.

REMIX always lives in the performance phase and delivers a solution, product, service, or experience. When you remix and perform, your audience is listening. Subsequently, when you listen deeply to your audience while they are listening to your remix, you will get fundamental input for the next version or iteration. The two sides of this cue are to deliver and to live. Most importantly, it is not just a remix, but a remix fuelled by the three cues JAMMIN', EMPATHY, and PERSONALITY in the challenge space: what people need, who we are and what fits our brand, and the creativity to combine this into something extraordinary.

In the Music Thinking Framework, you always end with a REMIX. This is the delivery part of the performance phase. While we as a company deliver at the end of the solution space, our audience listens in the challenge space. This creates the loop of iteration in our business and repeated delivery. This will eventually lead to living the brand by repeatedly remixing it based on personality, what people need, want, and buy — the endless loop of a sound business.

Are you still just playing the score?

In the SCORE chapter, we learned that the score is not the music, but when you deliver your experience, it is the moment to compare the outcome with the score. The insights on how people experience and listen to the remix might give you new insights for scoring. The input comes via EMPATHY (how did they listen; did they like it?) and PERSONALITY (does this support who we are and want to be as a brand?). The question is what and how do we have to adjust the score to get a better remix in the next possible iteration.

Here's a very practical example of this thinking: grab your smartphone and have a look at the general tab. Mine says software version 14.8, which means it is the 14th major iteration, with the 8th smaller iteration giving me the current performance.

Unfortunately, many assignments, ad hoc projects, and projects in crisis start with the REMIX cue. There is so much going on, and the time pressure is high. It is natural to first start remixing what you have and know and just make a new mix. So, when we start with the REMIX cue, it is essential to understand what the leading perspectives are and what the appropriate leadership positions are that guarantee the best remix in this phase.

Leading from different perspectives

Have a look at the Leadership Positions graphic. In Music Thinking there are different positions a leader can take to facilitate the right outcome. It is important to understand what the score is, what the dynamics are, and what kind of result is needed for your audience?

You should ask yourself the question: What kind of leadership and followership would I need? What possible positions and capabilities should the leadership style incorporate for the best result? Do you need

a composer who works on the score and changes it so that the players know exactly what to play, based on the composer's unique imagination to surprise the audience;

a master who mentors, coaches and, based on his function as a living role model, example, and personality, inspires and accompanies everyone to meet the best results;

a conductor who knows the score, the vision of the composer, and also knows the venue and the audience and has the knowledge and the authority to lead experts to the highest performance;

an improviser who works as a creative player in the middle of the music who can invent and play on the spot, engage others to play their very best, while also being the chief listener of the group and the changing audience;

a producer who knows the instrument's technicalities, the possibilities of all players, and the way the audience is listening; and who has the personality and power to change things so that everyone can be their best.

If you need *all the above*, then compare the five positions of Music Thinking leadership that every leader should know.

Are you playing jazz, classical music, hip hop, folk, EDM, or another style? It might matter because the way you listen might influence the way you lead.
And if your business, challenge, or programme is genre fluid – a mix of different styles – you might need a leader who can change positions and players who can lead and follow.

LEADERSHIP POSITIONS

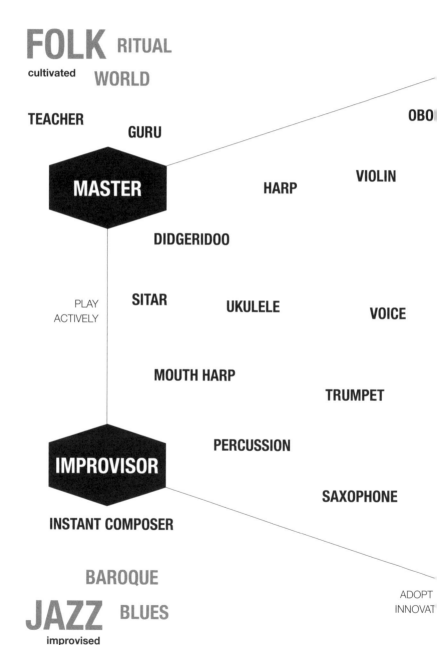

ADAPT &
CONSERVATE

CLASSICAL
interpreted

CELLO

CONCERT MASTER

BASSOON

CONDUCTOR

CLARINET

PIANO

BASS

COMPOSER

KEYBOARD

MAKE
NO
NOISE

SYNTHESIZER

GUITAR

PRODUCER

DRUMS

DJ   MIXER

RECORDING
ENGINEER

A&R MANAGER

EDM

HIP HOP

POP

ROCK

produced

Download the templates from musicthinking.com or take a piece of paper, fold it in the middle, and write REMIX on top of the fold.
Write 'to deliver' on the left and 'to live' on the right.

Use this cue when you are ready to deliver to your stakeholders. Collect and generate questions. Select possible instruments and activities that might help you to move forward.

Here is a suggestion of instruments that work well with this cue.

Realisation Platforms
Co-creation Platforms
Minimal Viable Product
High Fidelity Prototyping
Minimal Releasable Product
Quest for the Ultimate Remix
Living the Paradox
Feedback Loops
Live Testing

TO DELIVER

REMIX

TO LIVE

Questions to ask yourself:

Who in the organisation can play different roles and is accepted to take in different positions?

What positions should our leaders know and take?

How can we consistently deliver and continuously surprise our stakeholders?

Are we in a sprint or in a marathon?

Three steps in 60' **1.** Start solo and silent with your own template. 10'

2. Discuss in duos and share your thoughts, connect and collect. 20'

3. Share insights in full ensemble and make connections with the other cues. 30'

This is about ideas, information, opening up, sensing and collecting data from many sources.

to open — to sense
to explore — JAMMIN' — to create

And the driving force of creativity, exploration and creation based on the input from other cues.

to listen — EMPATHY — to understand

Empathy is the people-centred cue to see with the eyes of your stakeholders in their context and environment. Empathise and search for insights that matter. The two sides are listening and understanding.

to be — PERSONALITY — to become

The cue to work from the heart of your organisation. Work from your why and brand values to the holding space you provide for your stakeholders. That's why this cue has two sides: to be and to become.

to show — SCORE — to do

The cue to visualise your decisions in the way that everyone has a 'lead sheet' of how to operate. The two sides of this cue are to show and to do. This means you need to have a vision and clear instructions on how to reach this.

to learn — AGILITY — to change

The cue to decide how to work together in which constellations and when to do what. The two sides of this cue are to learn and to change. Together with Jammin', this is the realisation duo.

to deliver — REMIX — to live

The cue to getting it all together under the given circumstances based on the other cues. The two sides of this cue are to deliver and to live. There is a time when you have to deliver and to make iterations based on all the other cues.

musicthinking.com

Download this template from musicthinking.com

ACT IV

LET'S PLAY TOGETHER

Now that you have met all the cues, let's have a closer look at how they play together and how they are connected. For an overview, use the framework on the inside of the front flap.

Thinking from the perspective of one cue is the start of working with the framework. But just working with only one cue in isolation is worthless. The value of working with the framework is in the interconnection of the cues. Every cue comes to life in a direct relationship with one or more other cues. Sometimes in harmony, often in a friendly field of tension, or in a challenging paradox.

The cues build a system of flows that give output and receive input. For example, EMPATHY is giving *understanding,* and PERSONALITY gives *becoming,* as an output to SCORE. This means SCORE receives and shows the input and transforms it into a to-do for JAMMIN' and AGILITY. This is done continually in an ongoing iteration through all the cues. REMIX delivers it and brings it into an ongoing loop.

This is comparable to an analog synthesizer's input and output functions, where the output of a sine wave can influence other parameters like pitch, with the effect of a rising and falling pitch according to the shape of the sine wave. If the sine wave is connected to another input, like an amplifier, then the sound will be softer and harder

PLAY WITH ALL THE ELEMENTS

The Reactable is an electronic musical instrument
that enables everyone to experiment with sound,
change its structure and be creative in an engaging,
fun and visually appealing way. reactable.com

according to the same sine wave. So, the wave is the input for the next module. The 1972 ARP 2600 that Brian Eno and Jean Michel Jarre use is an example of this. The principle of the synthesizer is also used in an interactive workshop table, called the Reactable, where people can experience teamwork and co-creation with music and learn the effect of the interaction between input and output.

There are one-on-one relationships between two cues, like giving output and receiving input. For example

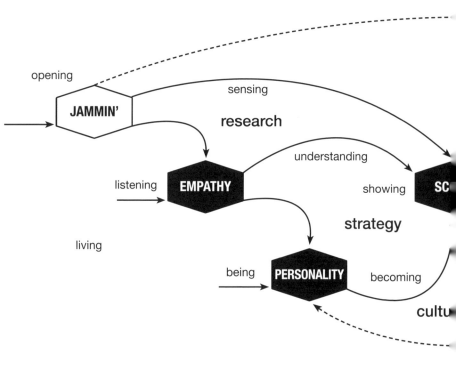

EMPATHY gives an understanding of the research on people and their context to show in the SCORE. When three cues are connected, they still have a one-on-one relationship, and they form a triangle with a thematic field.

Start with triangles for Change

All cues are bound in triangles, where they interact with at least two other cues. The triangles build themes like research, strategy, creativity, culture, production, and experiences for service, brand, and organisation.

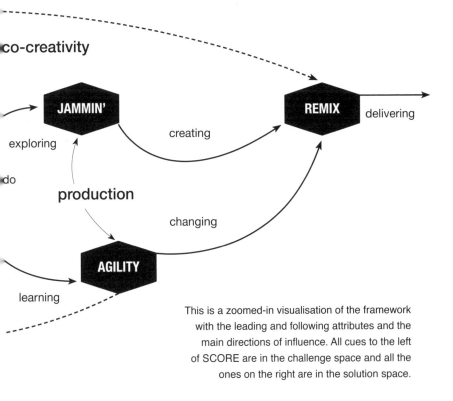

co-creativity

This is a zoomed-in visualisation of the framework with the leading and following attributes and the main directions of influence. All cues to the left of SCORE are in the challenge space and all the ones on the right are in the solution space.

So, instead of focussing on one cue as a start, you can also start with a theme. Let's have a look at the triangles step by step.

Research triangle: Every company that wants to understand what their customers really need has to continually develop research expertise to reveal the current state of knowledge. Starting new research and to sense the field for new signals comes from the JAMMIN' cue. In order to gain insights you also need the EMPATHY cue. You need to combine listening with your total capacity to quantitative and qualitative data and understanding and transforming the changing data. These gathered insights are only valid if you make it visual in the SCORE and share it with everyone involved as a possible solution to reveal what is going on. So, the systematic connection of the triangle formed by JAMMIN'-EMPATHY-SCORE will lead to proper research of insights and possibilities.

Strategy triangle: To work on the strategy requires two things: a familiar and mutual understanding of what people need, want, and would like to buy, and an understanding of what our organisation stands for (now and in the future) – EMPATHY and PERSONALITY. So, listening to and understanding stakeholders together with the awareness of being and becoming the brand must result in a 'to show' and then in a 'to do'. EMPATHY-PERSONALITY-SCORE will lead to an organisational design or new strategy where the needs of the potential audience and the organisation are levelled out and synthesised.

Culture triangle: The culture of an organisation is the result of all intentions, actions, and experiences. Culture is the outcome of the relationship between who you are, who you want to be, what you say, and how you act upon this. There is a feedback loop that gives extra output from the learning in AGILITY to the output generated by PERSONALITY to the SCORE. If this is not in flow, your brand and all the products and services you offer will fail at some point. Simon Sinek has developed an instrument – the Golden Circle – that connects the triangles: his Why, How, What distributes over PERSONALITY, AGILITY, SCORE.

As you can see PERSONALITY and SCORE share two triangles: the strategy triangle and the culture triangle. This reveals that there is an interrelation between strategy and culture.

Tip: Use the templates from the cue chapters for the following example.

Suppose you have a challenge in your company's culture. You might begin with the PERSONALITY cue and dive deeper into the *to be* part and use instruments like the Purpose or the Golden Circle, or listen to what people inside and outside the organisation say about you.

Then you look into the other side: *to become*. What should be the output for becoming? After that, do the same with SCORE; look into the showing part. How can you translate this into a doing that everybody can act upon? Then check AGILITY. How do people learn what *to do* and what should be changed by them or by the organisation?

Find patterns and see how they connect, how they complement or contradict each other. What are patterns of success? Make this visual and share and discuss it with your stakeholders.

Co-creativity triangle: Because creativity will flourish when sensing connects directly with exploration and co-creation to deliver, the creativity triangle can be used in different ways.

The direct link between JAMMIN' and REMIX will lead to rapid co-creation results without boundaries for short-term innovation projects, start-up try-outs, or future probing. The instrument Future Probing helps to sense signals of the future, rapid-prototyping experiences and making sense of them and apply them. In a start-up organisation, this will speed up the delivery cycle.

In a more mature or scaled-up organisation, it is essential to explore and create based on the output of EMPATHY and PERSONALITY that is written down in a SCORE.

To connect these two cues will slow down the execution of the delivery but it will add relevance and fit to what consumers want and what the brand stands for. This means we need to use creativity for a quick result and build up the muscle to connect all the cues repeatedly and continuously live the brand.

Connecting JAMMIN' and REMIX to SCORE will make it more meaningful because the creativity relates to the SCORE, which got input from EMPATHY, PERSONALITY, and maybe from the first JAMMIN'.

Production triangles

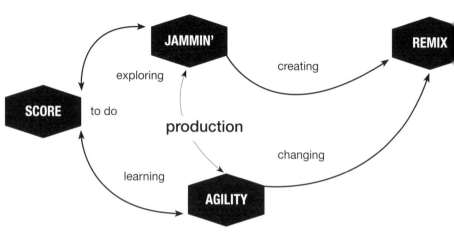

Zoom into the production area. All cues are in the solution space.

Let's have a look at the cues in the production triangles that are in the solution space. They consist of two intertwined Production triangles with JAMMIN' to explore and AGILITY to learn as the drivers for realisation from the SCORE's starting point and the endpoint REMIX to deliver.

As a diverging factor, JAMMIN' is exploring, and AGILITY is learning in parallel while they converge with creating and changing to the delivery.

SCORE-JAMMIN'-AGILITY are quality factors in exploring and looking for possibilities and learning the SCORE and how to interpret the *to do*. The arrow back to SCORE means that in some situations it should be possible to change the SCORE based on the learning and insights from exploration to realise the SCORE.

JAMMIN'-AGILITY-REMIX are working together in creating and changing their way for the next delivery.

Experience triangles

Suppose experience is the process of getting knowledge or skill from doing, seeing, hearing, recognising, perceiving, or sensing. In that case, we have three kinds of experiences in the framework. The experience while using a product or service, the experience you have, or have had, with a brand – this can incorporate different services – and the experience you have, or have had, while interacting with the organisation. In an ideal world, these experiences are seamlessly interwoven, but many companies have segmented this in silos like customer experience, marketing, brand department, and human resources.

A meaningful organisation with a strong brand and service needs to synthesise these experiences into one.

Three triangles generate extra output from experiences on three levels: product-service, brand, and organisation.

They all are connected to the REMIX cue because it is an interaction with a concrete delivery.

To better understand how the first iteration and delivery work – making it possible to experience this delivery – I have copied AGILITY and REMIX before the three cues in the challenge space: JAMMIN', EMPATHY, and PERSONALITY. This is the way the framework works when it iterates.

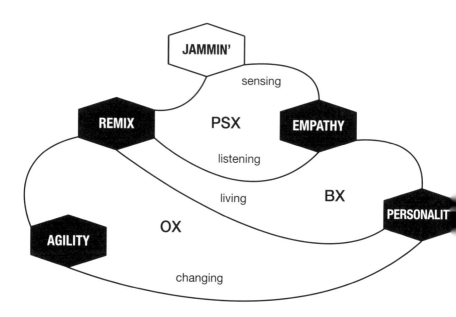

This is a rearranged visualisation with AGILITY and REMIX before the Challenge space. When we iterate for the first time, REMIX and AGILITY give input to JAMMIN', EMPATHY, and PERSONALITY, and they will give information again to SCORE.

Please take a moment to let this sink in; it is the basic idea of the flexible framework.

Product Service Experience (PSX)

REMIX, JAMMIN', EMPATHY – the experience of product and services is the experience with the output of REMIX regarding the usefulness and suitability of service, product, and consumer. The understanding of the service market fit and how people buy and use the service. This experience will be on the service only – for people who might not know the brand or people who use it for the first time. These experiences can also incorporate unintended use and lead to new output for creativity and change. Examples are Text messages (originally developed to let customers know about problems with their cell phone networks), Kleenex (intended for make-up removal), and WD-40 (designed to displace and repeal standing water to prevent corrosion in nuclear missiles).

A musical example: the song 'Vamos a la Playa' became a huge summer hit in discos all over Europe. However, the lyrics talk about an atom bomb detonation and a call to gather at the beach for rescue (few people understood the Spanish lyrics).

Brand Experience (BX)

REMIX, EMPATHY, PERSONALITY – the experience of products and services concerning the brand's promise. This is less about the usefulness (because a product can be helpful but still not fit people's expectations of the brand); it is about connecting and understanding the consumer and customer regarding the shared values and purpose of a brand. There are famous examples, like Apple and BMW, but let's not forget local or family-run businesses and B2B brands. They live their brand values directly in the interaction instead of advertising.

That is why local bands that live, breathe, and share the local culture are a solid and sustainable fit with their audience.

On a larger scale, Lady Gaga (with more than 80 million followers on Twitter) is close to her fans, whom she calls 'little monsters'.

Organisational Experience (OX)

What is it like to work together in an organisation? The triangle AGILITY-REMIX-PERSONALITY is the emotional experience of working in the tension field of what PERSONALITY communicates to AGILITY via SCORE. Via REMIX, the organisational experience connects again with PERSONALITY giving input to PERSONALITY via the delivered service. It is a loop where the culture influences the service and the service the culture. This leads us to the following questions:

'How does the tension of constantly focussing on a successful outcome relate with the brand values, purpose, and the service experience?', 'How can companies and their products and services we love at a particular time fail to connect their organisational experience with their renowned brand and product?'

Because we live in constant iterations and changes, the REMIX in the performance phase impacts the experience. We try to get it right the first time or we can create a culture of constantly iterating change and making the experience better. How we approach this will create a different dynamic on how the theme triangles and the cues interact. In this regard, all employees' leadership and followership skills must relate to the mechanics of the experiences and act upon them while delivering the service.

Three tracks through the framework
To start a project or a time-based assignment, we first need to understand what the Unanswered Question is. Ideally, you start with listening in the challenge space based on the Unanswered Question.

There are three tracks that lead you through the framework for your Unanswered Question:

1. Co-creativity Track
Start with JAMMIN' before SCORE for projects or workshops that focus on creativity, or in an orientation phase where the client is looking for 'new approaches' with no direct project link or a latent need for change. Cue order will be: JAMMIN', JAMMIN', REMIX, and then iterate and include SCORE. In a later iteration, EMPATHY, PERSONALITY and AGILITY will be connected.

2. Service Design Track
Start with EMPATHY for projects with a strong need for service design thinking, a change of audience behaviour,

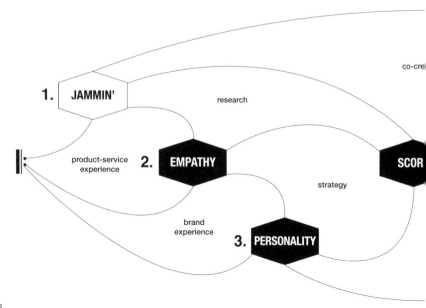

an unclear definition of the audience or innovation projects that focus on the current business model or innovations that are new to the organisation.

Cue order will be EMPATHY, SCORE, JAMMIN', REMIX. Iterate and include PERSONALITY and then later AGILITY.

3. Brand and Organisational Change Track

Start with PERSONALITY for organisational change projects or projects where there is a latent need for strategy or identity change and long-term innovation programmes.

Cue order will be PERSONALITY, SCORE, EMPATHY, SCORE, AGILITY, JAMMIN', REMIX.

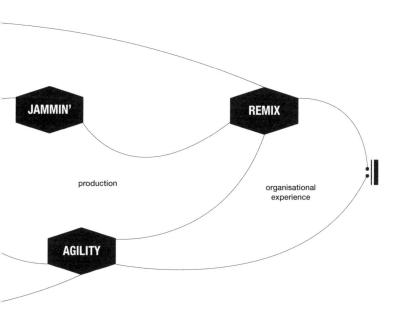

Daikokuji-Sasayama Komusō Shakuhachi   commons.wikimedia.org

ROLI Ltd 2020

The joy of learning a new instrument is a skill every leader should experience. Because it sets you back to the very beginning of listening, understanding, learning, trying, repeating, and eventually mastering. It gives you time to experience yourself in a learning process. Any instrument from electrical guitar to a violin is great to learn. Just follow your instinct, or choose one of these:

Shakuhachi if you are interested in sound meditation, a breathing ritual, learning a completely new way of scoring, experiencing music, and learning for personal improvement, then the Shakuhachi *Yuu* is a perfect instrument to start. For online lessons and info: hijirishakuhachi.com

Ukulele if you want quick results in playing and singing songs together with others. A concert ukulele is a good size to start because it is easier to handle.

Electronic instruments like ODD ball or ROLI BLOCKS combined with your smartphone. If you want to learn new sounds and interactions and if you are interested in experimentation and sound experiences that look 'cool'.

ACT V

EVERY BUSINESS IS DYNAMIC

Let's recap. In the Music Thinking Framework, the six cues JAMMIN', EMPATHY, PERSONALITY, SCORE, AGILITY, and REMIX are systemically connected and they give each other input and output. They do this with various instruments like Persona, Customer Journey, Systemic Mapping, Business Model Canvas, or the Golden Circle. The idea is to walk through the framework repeatedly from left to right and – iteration by iteration – improve the output and input via the instruments.

The cues and instruments live in the overarching phases Listen, Tune, Play, and Perform – with Listen being active in the other phases too.

While Listen and Play are the primary diverging phases that create choices, Tune and Perform are the converging powers that make choices for the current iteration using cues and instruments.
So, the phases are dynamic, flexible in time and intensity, and they overlap in multiple ways.

When we do things step by step, things seem to be easy. But what happens when the challenge space and the solution space merge and everything is happening simultaneously?

I have experienced many people struggling with the static use of the Double Diamond in Design Thinking and the three to five steps (when you google *Double Diamond* and click on images you will literally see different interpretations and visualisations).

Although unintentionally, many people use it as a fancy waterfall, doing nothing more than a single design sprint with the double diamond. In my experience, the last step of testing is part of performing and it is an opportunity to iterate. This makes it possible to review and adapt to the test results, listen better, and get new insights on how people use and understand the services. Remember, while you are performing (end of solution space), your audience is listening (beginning of the challenge space).

Because in real life this iteration occurs in many different ways. The phases Listen, Tune, Play, and Perform – or the steps of the double diamond – are stretched, squeezed, stamped, overlapped, and transformed. I call them dynamics. Please find some coloured variations of the dynamics in the back flap.

The way the cues connect to the instruments will affect the dynamics of the phases. That will depend on how long they last, on their volume, the amount of overlap, and the iteration speed. And because every leader, team, organisation, programme, project, or operation is different, we are likely to experience many different dynamics.

Sometimes over the period of a project, sometimes in specific timeframes like a sprint or a project phase.

In business we don't have a name for the different dynamics that can occur, so I would like to draw an analogy with music. Thus, we can start to see evolving and changing patterns that we can recognise, understand, explain, and transform into the area we are operating in.

Music is a very broad field: there is variety in genre, in the way of organisation, and in how people play together for a collective result. Here, I will draw parallels between several musical genre styles such as classical music, rock, pop, and jazz.

Let's have a closer look at some basic examples.

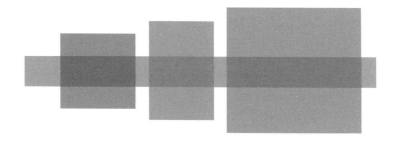

Classical: When performing classical orchestral music, there are clear steps taken before a performance. Based on continuous listening, the composer makes decisions and works these in a score. This is not just the sound idea but also an exact visual instruction for professional musicians trained on the instrument in question on what to do when. A conductor is accountable for the outcome. He has a vision of the score's interpretation and of how it will sound in the venue. During several rehearsals, he will coach the instrumentalists on how to bring it to life. The conductor syncs the players to this one sound during the performance by listening precisely to what is happening.

In project management, we would call this a waterfall: listen, compose, rehearse, and perform. The focus is on the highly trained experts and the proper execution of a given functionality or goal. If a particular expert is not available (sick, other), another expert with the same expertise can replace him or her.

The driver is the composition, and it is built for interpretation and correct execution in a given space for longer forms like symphony or opera.

Listening tip: Any symphony or opera by first-class orchestras like the Berlin or New York Philharmonic.

Jazz: There is no written score in free improvised music. There's only a general understanding to bend for a common result. Because there is no written score, there is nothing wrong as long as the actions fit the consensus of the players. The highly individual players agree on bringing their utmost concentration to create something unheard. Everything is happening simultaneously; it feels nonlinear, flexible, open-ended, democratic, and highly dynamic. The challenge space melts into the solution space. As an improviser, you are always performing.

If a player is not available, the replacement will have an impact on the collective outcome.

The driver is the tension between the improviser's personality and the will to create something new together. It is built for individual freedom, momentum, and innovation guided by collective listening for flexible time durations.

Listening tip: Art Ensemble of Chicago, Derek Bailey, Peter Brötzmann, Ornette Coleman's Free Jazz.

Pop: In pop music, a musician or band connects with a producer to deliver a product like an album. A player is engaged in executing a specific type of expertise in their own personal sound. Different variations, experiments and try-outs will be recorded and later discarded if not appropriate. The editing, mixing, and remixing is a substantial part of the production process.

The driver is the technological iteration built for impact on a given result, like radio play with a duration of three minutes or the capability of a medium like a cassette, single record, or album. The decline of physical media has not fundamentally changed this habit; the average pop playlist consists of songs of around three minutes.

Listening tip: Turn on your local radio or listen to the most popular playlists of your favourite streaming service.

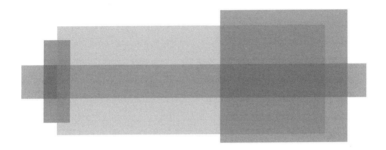

Rock: There are many variations of rock music. Let's use this pattern as an example: A band of maybe four players has found their genre and are experimenting, prototyping new things to push their boundaries in order to finally reach their unique sound and style. If they find their style and their fans will like this, they will not change it fundamentally.

For example, this is how U2 writes their songs: they come together and, during the rehearsal, find their sound. Bono, the singer, is singing in placeholder lyrics to match the feeling of the song. The actual words will come later. The band calls this technique of rapid prototyping 'bongolese'. When everything is done, the song is played live for the fans and eventually becomes fixed. This is second nature to the band. If a group member is not available (sick, leaves), the band breaks up or will look for an alternative that can fill in, which will sometimes lead to slight changes in the sound.

The driver is the consensus of the group members, and it is built for collective expression.

This approach comes close to group dynamics with the following phases: forming, storming, norming, performing, and adjourning. You can also find this pattern in a start up where co-founders leave or take different roles in the scale-up phase. While the band's core stays together, the scale-up is done around the group: band members are replaced with similar musicians. Still, management, record company, publishing, life equipment, and booking are added and define the way of working.

Listening tip: search for 'bongolese', and you will find a documentary on the 20th anniversary of the album Achtung Baby by U2. Bands like Rolling Stones, Queen, AC/DC, and Metallica work like this.

Musical styles and organisation styles

If you take a moment and think about the following questions, can you parallel or transform the underlying patterns to your endeavour? Which of the styles have an analogy with your organisation or business? How do the musical styles relate to departments like human resources, innovation hubs, sales, marketing, design, or young talent programmes?

And in what way could we compare this to organisations like multinational companies, private companies, non-governmental organisations, family-run businesses, start-ups, one-person companies, limited companies, and so on?

The idea of these analogies is not to get a one-on-one relationship between a band and a company but to learn from music and organisation patterns to reveal how we (could) work together.

As mentioned, there are close to 6000 genre styles listed on the *Every noise at once* website, not to mention the even bigger number of artists, bands, ensembles, etc.

Have a look at the inside of the back flap, here you will see a variety of the sheer endless possibilities of how the four phases including the cues and instruments can

GENRE STYLES IN SPRINTS

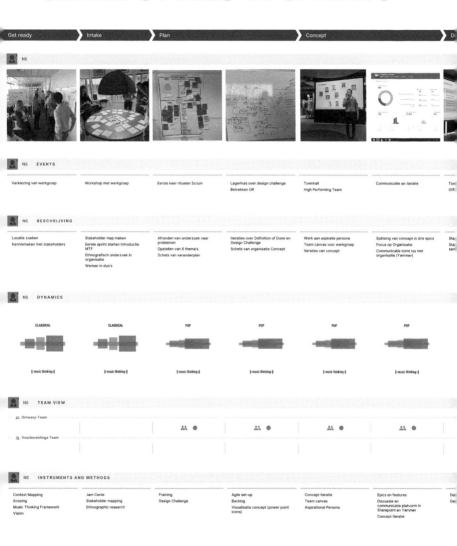

For an extensive transformation project in the railway industry, we visualised the different dynamics for every two-week sprint we had done. Even in hindsight, it was beneficial to understand

the different dynamics, what they meant, and what we could
learn for the next project or programme.

overlap. The variations on the exemplified dynamics are rather genre-fluid to get you into the mode of pattern recognition and making your own analogies.

Would you mind reading them as inspirations in how you would describe the dynamics of your project, team, sprint, or organisation?

Mixing dynamics

As you might imagine, the dynamics are not static. The dynamic of a team, organisation can change as quickly as the business itself. For example, you might plan a project the classical way, and while you think you are in the second phase, TUNE, you realise that you are already in jazz mode.

Your dynamic has changed, and the first thing that you should try to understand is what has caused the change:

What does this mean?

Is this experienced in the same way by all the stakeholders?

Is this a problem?

Is this something you need to change, or do you accept this and will you try to modify it in a possible next step to cool down and make it more transparent?

Because classical music is not better than jazz, or the other way round. There is no need to change as long as it feels good to proceed.

In order to understand dynamics, the best thing to do is to zoom out and see the whole field of operations. Then zoom in again and try to find the connecting cue and listen to what instruments are in play. Is everybody working with the same instruments in the same way?

Dynamics always go together with emotions. It's emotions that show the dynamics. So, it is crucial that we use the dynamics to show what is going on, compare it to the feelings, and determine if these emotions are the ones we want or whether it is possible to do interventions to change the dynamics.

The Unanswered Question check
After reading about the dynamics, you might start working on the Unanswered Question you defined when we began our journey so you can start to reveal and recognise dynamics and what they mean.

Jazzed-up business

Because the Listen phase goes through all the other phases, it is technically possible to start with REMIX. This is not ideal, but it is very likely to happen.

For example, suppose the question is 'helping with a concrete project' and it has a short time focus. In that case, your client or sponsor is so bound to the solution space and a short-term performance that it helps them to first try to understand what the SCORE is and then focus on JAMMIN' in combination with AGILITY to iterate a REMIX.

That approach will always indicate a jazz dynamic (a lot of things happening simultaneously), assuming that the score is not yet defined. There will be a lot of time-pressured interpretation and instant re-composing to a culture-defined outcome. It is comparable to JAMMIN' after SCORE in the 'repair' mode.

It is essential to negotiate a Listen phase, because this would be the first iteration after the delivery. The outcome of the Listen phase would affect EMPATHY, because it is a service or product experience.

It can also be connected to the PERSONALITY cue if the brand experience is important. In this way, it is important to define the insights of the experience and how the audience perceives the product, service, or brand and what might be a better approach or next step to make the organisational experience.

Warning: If it is impossible to do at least one iteration to listen and reflect on the three experiences you will stay in the unwanted vicious circle of delivery. Leaving listen and tune out of your loop.

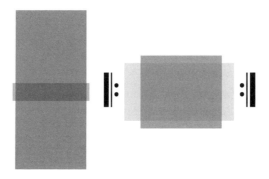

BACKSTAGE

ANALOGIES BEYOND THE METAPHOR

Good mathematicians see analogies. Great mathematicians see analogies between analogies.

Stefan Banach

Good musicians recognise patterns. Great musicians recognise patterns between patterns.

Good music thinkers recognise analogies. Great music thinkers act on analogies between analogies.

Christof Zürn

What do Albert Einstein (physicist), Bill Clinton (president), Jaron Lanier (computer scientist, futurist), Stephon Alexander (physicist), Charles Ives (insurance salesman, composer), Iannis Xenakis (architect, composer), Hans Reichel (font designer, luthier), Rodolfo Bonetto (designer), Jeff 'Skunk' Baxter (US security advisor) and Youssou N'Dour (minister, special ambassador) have in common?

All of them are creating extraordinary things in their field with music as a parallel companion. I would like to call them the **and-musicians** because they are famous for what they are doing, **and** they are musicians in some way.

This also goes for everyone I had a conversation with in The Power of Music Thinking podcast. Beautiful minds that can navigate in and between two fields. They go beyond the metaphor of just using musical terms to get a message across.

And-musicians work in different fields at the same time and they see patterns, relations and similes that inspire each other in transformative thinking in a new way. Where other people just know a quote or metaphor, they see the analogy, what it might mean in another system and they are able to play with that idea further.

I would like to close this book with some thoughts, triggers, and nudges about analogies. Analogies in music, business, organisations, society, or any other field. I feel this is important because it helps us sharpen our thinking and understanding of areas that seem to be unrelated at first sight. To be able to relate to them, transform them and make them prominent is a massive step in meaningful collaboration.

Composing is to symphonic music as improvising is to jazz.
This is an analogy. It tries to draw a relationship between composition and improvisation in terms of their ability to create music. If you hear this analogy, you have to transform one pattern (symphonic music and composing) to another pattern (jazz and improvisation). When you get deeper into this pattern, you might recognise more details of how they work, transfer these relations, and compare them with the relations in the other system.
In his book *The Physics of Jazz*, Stephon Alexander describes how he switched between the two worlds of music and science.

By reconnecting the disciplines of physics and music through analogy, we can begin to understand physics through sound. Stephon Alexander

Another example for working with the same pattern in two fields is the Philips Pavilion at the 1958 World's Fair in Brussels. It was a spectacular new building that included new forms of media and presentation and a challenging concrete construction that had never been done before. This architecture's inventor and chief designer was Iannis Xenakis (although it has often been wrongly attributed to Le Corbusier). Iannis Xenakis studied engineering and worked with Le Corbusier, but in his later years he became a famous composer who worked on the intersection of mathematics, technology, and sound.

His composition for big orchestra 'Metastasis' (1953) was a literal translation and transformation of the graphical sketches. The flat surfaces had the shape of hyperbolic paraboloids (the same shape as the Pringles snacks) like those used to model the musical 'masses' and swells of his string glissandi. Yet unlike many avant-garde composers of the 20th century who would not work with such a thing as a completed score, Xenakis notated every event in traditional notation so that professional classical musicians could play it from the score.

15. Bxd5

Chess Game for two saxophone orchestras by Igor Lunder at the
premiere performance during the World Saxophone Congress in Zagreb.

Organisational score that was created in the MICC workshops and interpreted and played by a jazz combo.

A comparable way of thinking is the research project MICC (Music, Innovation Corporate Culture, 2017) initiated by Wolfgang Stark, where teams in a company workshop were asked to draw a score of their organisation. Then a jazz band would play this score and interpret the graphical signs into music. The participants listened to the sound of their score as played by the musicians and recognised 'blind spots' that were present but could not be seen or articulated yet. The musicians translated the graphic patterns into sound, and the participants listened to the music and now recognised the sound patterns and transformed them into meaningful ways of their organisation.

So, it is essential to recognise the patterns and then transform them to understand them. It is literally working in two fields at the same time. Although we might not identify

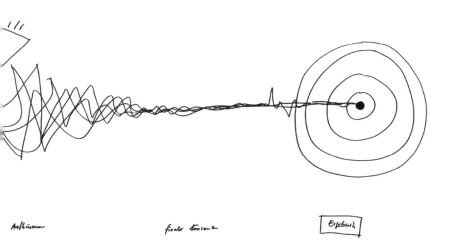

Aufbäumen   finale Sonieme   Erlebnis

something new in a specific system, we can start to see it in a new way when we recognise the pattern in another system and then transform this knowledge to the other system. The openness to identify patterns and the ability to transform them and develop them further is a strategy to connect intelligence and creativity and that will benefit every human endeavour.

There are many more examples that use harmony and resonance to reveal underlying patterns. I invite you to type *sonification experiments* into YouTube, lean back, and be inspired by all the experiments like the Chladni figures, sonification of plants to real-time audio, and visual display of the Coronavirus genome. I am curious what analogies they will ignite.

I encourage you to dive deeper into the endless world of everything music. Explore the field of listening, tuning, playing, and performing and live by the analogy:

Analogies are like stories; they need some time and development so that everybody can transfer the idea into the other system, anchor it, and play with it further.

On the following pages, I have listed some analogies for your inspiration. Dive into the field of these analogies and search for analogies for your endeavour.

Sound is to music as Music Thinking is to business and society.

Money is to rich as fitness is to health.

Black is to white
as off is to on.

Composing is to symphonic music as improvising is to jazz.

Conducting is to classical music as producing is to hip hop.

Buying is to vinyl as subscribing is to streaming.

_____ is to

_____

as

_____ is to

_____ .

SOUND BITES

TO TAKE HOME

As a summary for every chapter, here are some sound bites to use in conversations, as an email signature or as a guiding principle. All quotes are from the author unless otherwise noted.

Prologue
Followers can be leaders, and leaders become followers.

The universal power of music
If you see a pattern in one system, it is easy to see it in another system.

A Framework Based on Music Principles
The Listen phase is active in all other phases. That is because our ears are 'always on'; they continuously receive information – like a business is getting quantitative and qualitative data all the time.

The Unanswered Question gives a company more space to explore what exactly is going on. It also helps to connect short-term and long-term thinking about whether an iteration, innovation, or transformation is needed.

Take the Cue-train

Music Thinking = JASPER

JAMMIN', AGILITY, SCORE, PERSONALITY, EMPATHY, and REMIX.

Each of the six cues has two interwoven elements. A leading and a following side. One incorporates the other.

The more open you are, the more likely you are to have more ideas when you hear an idea. Openness is a prerequisite for creativity and intelligence – connecting new things with other new things and known things.

It is hard to change when your purpose is single minded and focussed only on money. For change you need to know who you are and who you want to be.

It is not fake it until you make it, but make it until you be it.

The score is not the music, and the strategy is not the service.

Score can be two things: a pilot's dashboard and a musical score with enough detail to give direction and synchronise all the different perspectives.

All the choices that we make in scoring our business will have a direct influence on the dynamic of interactions and flow.

The best advice for any organisation is to make scoring a habit.
In an organisation, everybody needs the training to be an instant composer and to quickly share the level of understanding when there is no score or when the score is less detailed.

Don't just play the SCORE. Explore first how you can bring to life what is intended in the SCORE.

Co-creation must be inclusive. Everybody has the same influence on the outcome, whether playing actively or listening profoundly while holding the space for the others.

If what is written in the score does not fit the capability of the players and the current system, then it needs a learning organisation to change it and a leadership that is helping to learn instead of trying to teach.

In music from approximately nine musicians, you need a conductor to synchronise and give the cues. With less than nine, one or more players will collectively sync and give cues.

Scale-up means seeing the whole field like a festival. Imagine a festival site with all its different stages and the backstage area with all the necessary means to make the festival a success.

Great duo partners don't just play together: They listen, tune, play, and perform while initiating new perspectives and amplify each other's possibilities.

When you listen deeply to your audience while they are listening to your remix, you will get fundamental input for the next version or iteration.

In Music Thinking, there are different positions a leader can take to facilitate the right outcome. Composer, Master, Conductor, Improviser, Producer, and Soloist.

The best thing to do to understand dynamics is to zoom out and see the whole field of operations. Then zoom in again and try to find the connecting cue and listen to what instruments are in play.

Backstage

Good musicians recognise patterns.
Great musicians recognise patterns between patterns.

Good music thinkers recognise analogies.
Great music thinkers act on analogies between analogies.

PLAYLISTS

JAMMIN' before SCORE

The Unanswered Question
Charles Ives
Lear
Pauline Oliveros & others
Exercises in Free Improvisation
Vladimir Horowitz
Ascension
John Coltrane
Dark Star
Grateful Dead

PERSONALITY

Move
Miles Davis
So What
Miles Davis
Milestones
Miles Davis
In Silent Way
Miles Davis
Pharaoh's Dance
Miles Davis

EMPATHY

Feeling Good
Nina Simone
We Are The World
U.S.A. for Africa
Mai Nozipo
Kronos Quartet, Dumisani Maraire
Nocturnes, Op9, No2
Frédéric Chopin
Little Wing
Jimi Hendrix

SCORE

In C
Terry Riley
The King of Denmark
Morton Feldman
Treatise
Cornelius Cardew
Helikopter Streichquartett
Karlheinz Stockhausen
4'33"
John Cage

JAMMIN' after SCORE

Pre-Performance Remark
Leonard Bernstein
Variations … Monteverdi
Art Ensemble of Chicago
Goldberg Variations (1955)
Glenn Gould, Bach
Goldberg Variations (1981)
Glenn Gould, Bach
Tenor Madness
Sonny Rollins, John Coltrane

AGILITY

Circle Song
Bobby McFerrin
Seven Nation Army
The White Stripes
Serenade
Sir Roland Hanna Trio
Come Together
The Beatles
Paint It Black
The Rolling Stones

REMIX

Amen Brother
The Winstons
Funky Drummer
James Brown
Good Times
Chic
Rapper's Delight
The Sugarhill Gang
My Guitar
DJ Kool Herc

PODCAST EPISODES

Rules of engagement
with Jim Kalbach

A Sound Facilitation Business
with Gerry Scullion

The Jazz Process to innovation
with Adrian Cho

Multi-sensory storytelling
with Jasper Udink ten Cate

The Thrills of Business
with Padraic McMahon

Cross-pollination in leadership
with Ilkka Mäkitalo

Music and the Brain
with Artur Jaschke

Deep listening
with Sharon Stewart

Innovation patterns and improvisation in organisations
with Wolfgang Stark

Music as a Catalyst for Change
with Nifemi Aluko

Blend sound science with sound art to make sound decisions
with Steve Keller

A mindset for entrepreneurship, leadership and design
with Michael Hendrix and Panos Panay

Blockchain Philosophy and Collaborative Transformation for Change
with Roy Scheerder

Get the latest episode and subscribe.

Podcast Page

THE SOUND OF EVERYTHING

Spotify has nearly 6000 different genre styles they are tracking.

One song from every genre Spotify is currently tracking.

It is a playlist with approximately 400 hours!

A KIND OF GLOSSARY

Like in music, there is a nearly endless number of instruments in business. Music Thinking connects canvases, tools, and approaches from various fields and combines them for meaningful collaboration. The idea is to pick what fits best with the way you want to play, combine the instruments with the cues and see that they are consistent. And everybody needs to know how to play the instrument. Please keep in mind that mastering an instrument needs hard work, training, and experience.

If you want to dive deeper into instruments, I recommend the following sources:
- Service Design www.thisisservicedesigndoing.com
- Branding www.martyneumeier.com/brand-az-book
- Organisation www.presencing.org/resource/tools

In addition, I'd like to show you some personal thoughts and best practices on the selected instruments I am using.

DEEP LISTENING
The term Deep Listening was coined by composer and improviser Pauline Oliveros as a result of a concert recorded in an underground cistern in 1988. The Deep Listening Institute organises retreats and trainings to inspire trained and untrained performers to practice the art of listening and responding to environmental conditions. www.deeplistening.org

Otto Scharmer uses the same term to explain his four levels of listening: downloading, factual, empathic, and generative. In a video, he explains the 'core skill for all domains of professional mastery' with the example of the conductor Zubin Mehta. On the website, you'll also find a tool to monitor your daily listening levels. www.presencing.org/resource/tools/listen-desc

CONTEXT MAPPING
Many meetings and projects fail because we only focus on what we should do instead of visualising everything related. It is essential to map all the different perspectives, including no-go areas, to see a field where all the possibilities are listed.

Then, it is crucial to decide together what to focus on.

QUESTION STORMING
Like brainstorming with ideas, you can do a question storming to come up with the right question to generate the right ideas.

LEADERSHIP & FOLLOWERSHIP
There is no leadership without followership, and the other way round. You can experience and learn this when you go to a concert. If it is classical music, try to go to a rehearsal: it will help you to understand the music much better. I highly recommend concerts with free improvisation because they allow you to experience the instant composing and structuring of the performance.

PURPOSE
Many organisations don't understand the difference between a purpose and a goal. A purpose is connected to your values: why and how you do things. A goal is to deliver successful services and products based on your purpose. Just making money is a goal without a purpose.

OGSM
Objectives, goals, strategies, and measures (OGSM) is a goal-setting and action plan framework, often on one page, used in strategic planning. Like any framework, it depends on how it connects with the company's purpose and values and fit the audience's purpose and values.

BACKLOG
A backlog is a list of items with the most important one at the top of the list. If your team works agile, management should too. It gives you the possibility to combine listening with scoring.

SYSTEMIC MAPPING
In order to understand a system, you need to map cause and effect from – and on – the players in the system. Thus, you can visualise how the variables and interactions influence the dynamics and emergent behaviour. That allows you to identify the leverage points for possible interventions. www.systemic-design.org

STAKEHOLDER MAPPING
A stakeholder mapping should always show the perspective of a human being with attributes and behaviours related to the challenge. So instead of using 'customers' as a stakeholder, use differentiators like 'impulse

shopper' and 'purpose-driven buyer'. Your challenge or Unanswered Question should be in the middle of the map. The closer a stakeholder is to the centre, the more influence it has on the challenge. If you don't know your stakeholders in detail, start with researching or mapping your challenge's 'ecosystem'.

TARGET GROUP

A target group is the description of a range of potential customers and consumers a company wants to reach and influence, based on market trends, segmented on quantitative data. It is used to quantify potential investment and return on that investment.

QUICK PROFILES

Profiles, quick profiles, or decision-making profiles are assumptions based on educated guesses. A profile represents the customer, consumer, or user. If there is no research, use quick profiles to make a version 0.1 to move forward. This can be validated later and iterated to personas (after quantitative and qualitative research).

REALITY PERSONA

Personas are detailed archetypal descriptions of typical members of a target group. A persona is the presentation and translation of all sorts of data, facts, and information into one practical format (a poster, for example). Reality personas are based on facts from research, they are updated and validated regularly, and they are related to the sources (quantitative and qualitative). A reality persona is data storytelling to take actions. A reality persona needs a date, a version number, and list of sources.

Use the persona like a mask to put on when you think and look from the perspective of a person with specific attributes, needs, and behaviours.

JOURNEY MAPPING

A journey is the experience of a person. That's why a journey mapping should always start with a certain (reality) persona and their specific attributes. Otherwise, it is just a process that will foster inside-out thinking.

JOURNEY OPERATIONS

Journeys can take place on different levels and details. Think about zooming in from country to city to street level. Agile organisations need this to better synchronise their operations based on different levels of insight. www.journeymapoperations.com

BRAND BOOK

Everyone in an organisation should understand what the organisation